VERSAILLES

AN ALEXIS GREGORY BOOK

GÉRALD VAN DER KEMP

MEMBRE DE L'INSTITUT
INSPECTEUR GÉNÉRAL DES MUSÉES NATIONAUX
CONSERVATEUR EN CHEF
DES MUSÉES DE VERSAILLES ET DES TRIANONS

VERSAILLES

PARK LANE

New York

New edition 1981
after restoration of the King's Bedchamber
and the Hall of Mirrors.

First published in French in 1977 by Editions d'Art Lys, Versailles
© 1978 by Editions d'Art Lys, 2 bis Passage Toulouse, Versailles
English language translation Copyright © Editions d'Art Lys, 1978

This edition is published by Park Lane,
a division of Crown Publishers, Inc.

a   b   c   d   e   f   g

Library of Congress Cataloging in Publication Data

Kemp, Gérald Van der.
  Versailles.
  Bibliography: p.
  Includes index.
  1. Versailles.   I. Title.
NA7736.V5K4613   708'.4'366   78–8248
ISBN   0–517–334895

Printed and bound in Italy

CONTENTS

The
Main
Gateway

The transformation of Louis XIII's modest hunting lodge at Versailles into the Sun King's Palace was the result of a combination of exceptional circumstances, both political and religious in nature.

When his father died in 1643, Louis XIV was five years old. His mother, Anne of Austria, was Queen Regent and governed with the help of her prime minister, Cardinal Mazarin. The nobility and parliaments attempted to regain the privileges taken from them by Cardinal Richelieu, and as a result the ruinous civil war called the Fronde broke out. In the end, the country was saved only by the tenacity of Anne of Austria and the cunning of Mazarin.

Louis XIV was to recall this troubled period all his life, and could never erase the memory of the Parisians invading his apartments in the Palais Royal, and that of the sudden flight of the royal family to the château of Saint-Germain-en-Laye on an icy winter's day. His distrust of Paris and of the nobility never left him.

When peace returned, the King therefore decided to settle some distance from the city in the château of the Tuileries with its magnificent gardens laid out

A trophy
from the
Hall of Mirrors

by Le Nôtre. But even the Tuileries was too vulnerable and Louis XIV went a step further by moving to the château of Saint-Germain-en-Laye, where Jules Hardouin-Mansart and André Le Nôtre collaborated in creating sumptuous embellishments, though little of these remains today.

Saint-Germain was near Versailles and, at the time of his liaison with the blonde Louise de la Vallière, Louis XIV began to house his mistresses in the château of Versailles, rebuilt by Philibert Le Roy in 1631. The façade was decorated by Louis le Vau with bricks and stone, sculpture, wrought iron and gilt lead. Le Nôtre took the design for the gardens by Boyceau and Menours and gave them greater breadth and dignity — and then the fountains began to play.

In 1668, Louis XIV adopted Le Vau's project to enlarge the château on the gardens side by enclosing it in an envelope of stone which would contain the King's and Queen's apartments, placed symmetrically to the north and south. And there, on the park side, the steep French roofs were abandoned in favor of Italian style flat roofs with parapets. Thus the spirit of the Louis XIII château is retained on the city side, but on the park side Le Vau relinquished brick, used only stone, and decorated the three floors with the traditional orders. The inspiration is certainly Italian, but baroque embellishments have been eliminated in favor of a sober and harmonious structure which is the classical French version.

With the work of Le Vau, of François d'Orbay and, later, of Jules Hardouin-Mansart, the château of Louis XIII became an immense palace with a west façade extending for over 2,000 feet. In returning to the sources of antiquity, French architecture was given a new lease of life which could be called a Second Renaissance, the influence of which spread throughout Europe, from Saint-Petersburg in Russia to Caserta in Italy.

There is no doubt that no period was more fruitful in every realm of Art and Thought. An unbelievable flowering of genius appeared at that time: Pascal, Corneille, Molière, Racine, La Fontaine, the Marquise de Sévigné, Saint-Simon, not forgetting the painters, like Le Brun, and the sculptors such as Coysevox and Girardon. A new art of living appeared, customs and manners became much more refined, and Versailles set the tone, so that someone living at the Court of France could be recognized by his way of speaking alone.

In order to keep closer watch over the nobility, the King tightened his links with it by raising his Court to a level of importance and prestige it had never previously reached, even under François I. By means of a rigid social code, l'etiquette, each subject had his place precisely defined in relation to the King and to the members of the royal family. The ladies of the Court always took first place. The King would bow to a princess, but, so great was his courtesy that he would never forget to take his hat off to the humblest of his chambermaids.

This, then, was the exceptional context in which the Versailles where Louis XIV settled permanently in 1682 was created. The power of French royalty was then at its zenith and the Monarchy of Divine Right triumphed and was embodied in the splendour of Versailles. Henceforth, the Kings of France took precedence over all the other sovereigns of Europe.

The seventeenth century was still imbued with the mythology which the Renaissance had again made fashionable and for this reason the architects, painters and sculptors quite naturally took their inspiration from the mythological themes of Ovid's *Metamorphoses* to create, at Versailles, a sort of Palace of the Sun. The King had chosen the sun as his emblem and, thus identified with Apollo, he became, at Versailles, the master of light, warmth and life and the victor over the forces of evil. Louis XV and Louis XVI carefully respected their ancestor's heritage and the transformations and embellishments they brought to Versailles in no way destroyed the harmony of this symbolism.

The pairing of Apollo and the sun, taken from the *Metamorphoses* and the Graeco-Latin mythological poems, was restored, by a stroke of genius, to nature itself, to its waters, woods, flowers, seasons and days. Here, the spirit of the ancient fable becomes reality, embodied as much in the inevitable order of nature as in the ideal that was always central to the royal scheme, the whole reaching its climax in the chapel, with the crowning of the supreme truth, Christ, the unique and unfailing Light of heaven and earth.

On the advice of Colbert, and with the precise aim of encouraging the development of French trade, Louis XIV had his courtiers live in unheard of luxury, and he decided that his château should be given permanent furnishings, something which had never been done before. Thus a set of furnishings of fabulous beauty and richness was created. A halt was put to the importation of mirrors from Venice, tapestries from Flanders and brocades from Italy, and preference was given instead to those produced at the royal Manufactories founded by Colbert. The manufacture of these products was strictly controlled and their quality made them sought after throughout Europe. This is how the Manufactories of Saint-Gobain for mirrors, Lyons and Tours for silks and brocades and the Gobelins and Savonnerie for tapestries and carpets earned their remarkable reputation.

Le Brun was placed in charge of everything concerning the decoration and furnishing of the royal residences; nothing escaped him, whether the drawing for a statue, the decoration of a ceiling, or the design of one of the solid silver pieces of furniture carved for the State Apartment.

With Boulle, French cabinet-making attained the pinnacle of its reputation and the furniture commissioned by Louis XIV, Louis XV and Louis XVI was to reach new heights in quality, elegance and beauty.

A hymn to the ruling power of light, Versailles is truly the Palace of the Sun, a poem of stone, greenery and water, the finest work in every sense and the most representative of the French seventeenth century. One single idea dominates, without, however, overshadowing the rest. Nothing in the imagination or the expression of truth is left to chance. Not only the eyes, but also the soul, the heart, the imagination, the intelligence are involved. Only a simple symbolical system, which our modern, technical, urban civilization must learn again, was needed. Versailles is a poem linking antiquity with the present and an admirable attempt at a synthesis crowned by the glory of God.

The illustrations which make up this book cannot pretend to depict this magnificence in its entirety, nor can the accompanying commentary retrace the glorious history of Versailles... that would take five volumes. But we hope that they will give some idea of the unceasing battle waged since the last war to restore to Versailles some of the brilliance of its youth. Of course, Versailles will never again know the luxury of yesteryear. Nevertheless, perseverance, effort, persuasion and generosity have joined forces to reveal the Salon d'Hercules, the King's Private Suite, the Queen's Bedchamber, the drawing rooms of the Grand Trianon and Marie-Antoinette's apartment in the Petit Trianon... and tomorrow it will be the turn of Louis XIV's Bedchamber and the Hall of Mirrors.

These, then, are the pictures, simply offered for reflection and contemplation, like an invitation to reverie which is the greatest luxury of our time.

Gérald Van der Kemp

*Versailles, december fifth,
nineteen hundred and seventy-six.*

Plans of the château

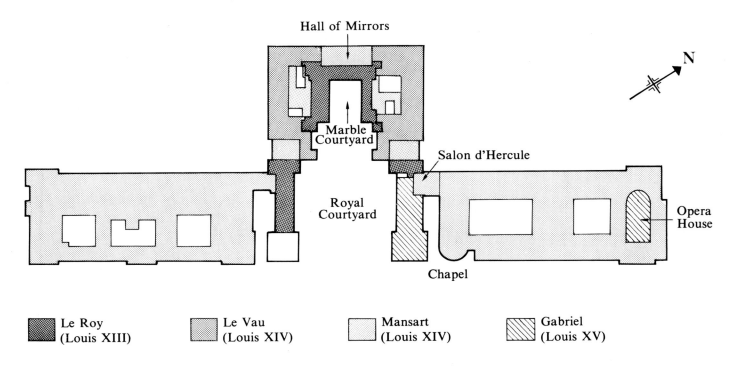

Hall of Mirrors

Marble Courtyard

Royal Courtyard

Salon d'Hercule

Opera House

Chapel

N

Le Roy (Louis XIII) Le Vau (Louis XIV) Mansart (Louis XIV) Gabriel (Louis XV)

THE BUILDING OF VERSAILLES

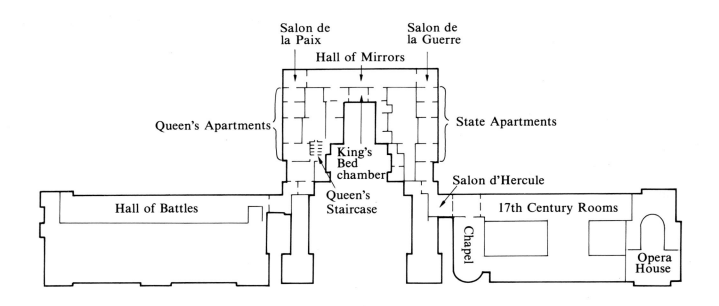

Salon de la Paix

Salon de la Guerre

Hall of Mirrors

Queen's Apartments

State Apartments

King's Bed chamber

Queen's Staircase

Salon d'Hercule

Hall of Battles

17th Century Rooms

Chapel

Opera House

PLAN OF THE FIRST FLOOR

The King's Private Suite lies between the King's Bedchamber and the State Apartments
The Queen's Private Suite lies behind the Queen's Apartments.

Genealogical table

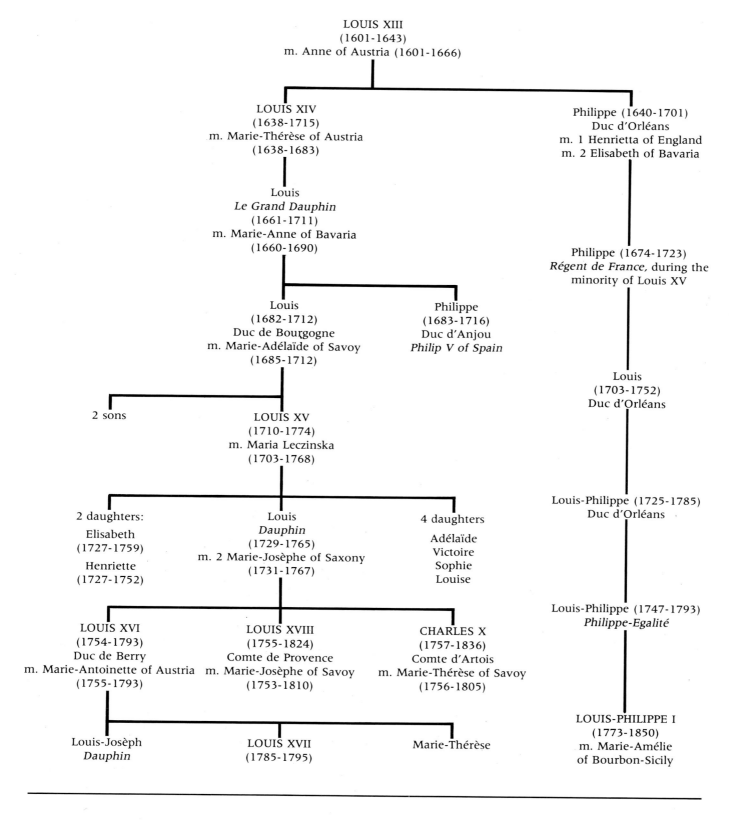

LOUIS XIII
(1601-1643)
m. Anne of Austria (1601-1666)

LOUIS XIV
(1638-1715)
m. Marie-Thérèse of Austria
(1638-1683)

Philippe (1640-1701)
Duc d'Orléans
m. 1 Henrietta of England
m. 2 Elisabeth of Bavaria

Louis
Le Grand Dauphin
(1661-1711)
m. Marie-Anne of Bavaria
(1660-1690)

Philippe (1674-1723)
Régent de France, during the
minority of Louis XV

Louis
(1682-1712)
Duc de Bourgogne
m. Marie-Adélaïde of Savoy
(1685-1712)

Philippe
(1683-1716)
Duc d'Anjou
Philip V of Spain

Louis
(1703-1752)
Duc d'Orléans

2 sons

LOUIS XV
(1710-1774)
m. Maria Leczinska
(1703-1768)

Louis-Philippe (1725-1785)
Duc d'Orléans

2 daughters:
Elisabeth
(1727-1759)
Henriette
(1727-1752)

Louis
Dauphin
(1729-1765)
m. 2 Marie-Josèphe of Saxony
(1731-1767)

4 daughters
Adélaïde
Victoire
Sophie
Louise

Louis-Philippe (1747-1793)
Philippe-Egalité

LOUIS XVI
(1754-1793)
Duc de Berry
m. Marie-Antoinette of Austria
(1755-1793)

LOUIS XVIII
(1755-1824)
Comte de Provence
m. Marie-Josèphe of Savoy
(1753-1810)

CHARLES X
(1757-1836)
Comte d'Artois
m. Marie-Thérèse of Savoy
(1756-1805)

Louis-Josèph
Dauphin

LOUIS XVII
(1785-1795)

Marie-Thérèse

LOUIS-PHILIPPE I
(1773-1850)
m. Marie-Amélie
of Bourbon-Sicily

REIGNS OF THE BOURBON KINGS:

Louis XIII (1610-1643)
Louis XIV (1643-1715)
Louis XV (1715-1774)
Louis XVI (1774-1792)

Louis XVII titular king only (1792-1795)
Louis XVIII (1814-1824)
Charles X (1824-1830)
Louis-Philippe (1830-1848)

The wings
of Louis XIII's
château

14

THE CHATEAU

The
Marble
Courtyard

15

« *Nous sommes à tes yeux, Passant, trois Avenues*

D'ormes à quatre rangs, et bien entretenues;
Louis nous fit planter au plus juste cordeau;
Aboutissans en ligne au superbe Palais ».

(Monicart)

The grand avenues of Saint-Cloud, Paris and Sceaux meet at the Place d'Armes, from where they radiate out through the whole city of Versailles.

After passing through the gateway, crowned with the Arms of France in glittering gold, the visitor enters the Great Courtyard. Flanked by Ministry buildings, it used to end, until the Revolution, at a second gilded gateway where the present equestrian statue of Louis XIV stands, commissioned by King Louis-Philippe in 1837 from the sculptors Cartellier and Petitot.

Then comes the Royal Courtyard, reserved for the lords who had the right to the "Honours of the Louvre"; they alone had the privilege of entering by carriage.

The Marble Courtyard was separated from the preceding one by several steps which prevented anyone from entering by horse and carriage. The buildings that frame it correspond to Louis XIII's château which, following Louis XIV's wishes, Le Vau and Mansart altered very little here.

In this spot where the centuries have left their dust, let us imagine the charm and gaiety of these buildings at a time when the stone was golden, the brick red, and the iron and lead covered with gold-leaf.

The
château
courtyards

16

The Great Courtyard,
the equestrian statue of Louis XIV,
the Royal Courtyard

The Ambassadors' Staircase

Conceived by Le Vau as a triumphal entrance to the King's State Apartments, the Ambassadors' Staircase was built by François d'Orbay. Charles Le Brun, with the help of Adam Van der Meulen, expressed here the whole range of his talent.

After passing through the gates, gilded by Delobel, visitors would cross a vestibule to the marble staircase. A huge flight of steps led to the first landing, the wall of which contained a niche with a fountain surmounted by a bust of the King. From there, two symmetrical stairways led to the Salons of Venus and Diana. Completed in 1678, this wonderful work was destroyed in 1752, and thus the only entrance worthy of the State Apartments was lost, the place where so many sumptuous processions of ambassadors had gathered while violins, flutes and oboes resounded.

Jean Warin: bust of
Louis XIV, from the
central niche of the staircase

18

Model of the
Ambassadors'
Staircase

19

The Lower Vestibule of the Chapel stands on the site of what was one of the great curiosities of Versailles during Louis XIV's youth, the grotto of Tethys. This remarkable construction, which held the famous group by Girardon "Apollo tended by nymphs" (now in the gardens), was destroyed in 1685.

The vestibule is divided into three bays by a series of handsome Ionic columns arranged in pairs.

While one might consider this to be a room of only secondary importance, its décor is no less majestic and beautiful. The white of the stone sets off the multicolored marble and throws into relief the great gilded doors of the chapel.

A bas-relief by Puget, depicting "Alexander and Diogenes", once adorned this room. In the nineteenth century, Louis-Philippe had the idea of placing here the marble bas-relief by Coustou which Louis XV had commissioned for the Salon de la Guerre and which illustrated the crossing of the Rhine by Louis XIV's armies.

Lower Vestibule
of the Chapel, with
bas-relief by Coustou

The entrance
to the
Royal Chapel

The Royal Chapel

God and religious matters were always at the forefront of Louis XIV's mind. In this, the King showed his loyalty to his ancestors.

He remembered that he had inherited the throne from Saint Louis and that his father had dedicated his country to the Virgin.

His piety was beyond reproach. To his enemies it was the sign of an inexplicable bigotry. "The King never missed Mass save once in his life", the Duc de Saint-Simon was to note, "in the army on the day of a long march, nor any day of fast save for a true and very rare impediment".

As the new century was about to dawn, the Sun King decided that the architects had not given God his due in the palace. However, it was not an ideal time to begin new construction work. France had been weakened after a war in which she almost lost everything, and she would soon have to take up arms again and bleed as never before to retain the kingdom of Spain for one of France's grandsons, the only descendant of Louis XIV whose line has not yet been extinguished.

Voltaire reveals that Madame de Maintenon was at that time most preoccupied by the poverty of the people, of which Racine had painted such a dark picture. "She did everything in her power to oppose the magnificent chapel which the King had built at Versailles", writes Mademoiselle d'Aumale, "because

Bas-relief on the main altar: pietà by Antoine Vassé

Marble floor in the nave

the poverty of the people was great at that time and she also believed that Versailles would no longer be the Court residence". To no avail. On 8th January 1699, Mansart was made Superintendent of Buildings. He thus had easy access to the King. The architect knew of his sovereign's passion for buildings. "He pestered him", comments Saint-Simon, "with projects which incurred the greatest expense." As far as architecture was concerned, the Sun King knew what he wanted, and, here, it was to offer God the finest temple possible.

Mansart did not live to enjoy the praise his chapel inspired. He died suddenly in 1708, a victim of his greedy appetite, as Saint-Simon reveals. Since the building was not yet complete, his brother-in-law, Robert de Cotte, was entrusted with the task of finishing it.

On 25th April 1710, the Marquis de Dangeau wrote in his diary that, after hearing Mass in the former chapel, the King entered "the new chapel and had a motet sung, to

The
royal
gallery

The Lady Chapel
with painting by
J.-B. Sauterre

hear the effect of the music''. Louis XIV expressed his satisfaction and, on 5th June, the edifice was consecrated by Cardinal de Noailles, Archbishop of Paris.

The new chapel was dedicated to Saint Louis, King of France. We touch here on the complexity of a period which prided itself on its classicism and yet did not reject certain aspects of the Middle Ages, present almost everywhere here. For example, in Louis IX's initials set in the marble mosaic of the floor; on the front of the altar where the sculptor, Antoine Vassé, sculpted with the greatest delicacy in gilded bronze the pietà of Mary receiving the body of her Son. Like the Sainte-Chapelle in Paris, this edifice has a gothic structure with two storeys, and the space is enclosed by Corinthian columns resting on massive pillars. The high transparent stained glass windows are a reminder of the cathedrals. And how can words describe the sumptuous organ loft designed by de Cotte and executed by the finest artists?

The
main altar and
the organ loft

The
chapel
vault

Contemporary descriptions of the chapel, reflecting opinions of the period, dwell less on the finely carved white stone reliefs which arouse our admiration today, than on the large paintings of the ceiling, the themes of which are all dedicated to the Holy Trinity.

The ceiling of the nave is divided into three compartments framed by paintings of architecture by Philippe Meusnier. In the center is the "Eternal Father in his glory", by Antoine Coypel. He is surrounded by his heavenly court and depicted as an old man from whom emanate "rays of light which illuminate the whole ceiling". On the royal gallery side, we see the "Descent of the Holy Spirit onto the Apostles", by Jean Jouvenet. With the years, the talent of Charles de Lafosse was confirmed, as the "Resurrection of Christ" adorning the cupola of the apse testifies. We see, "in a fine landscape Christ in the skies, painted with a brilliance and majesty as worthy of a God triumphing over death as the works of man can be".

Before dying, the old Sun King was able to congratulate himself on having offered to God, despite every obstacle, a magnificent testimony of his faith.

To his ancestors, he also bequeathed an edifice which he secretly wanted to be the sanctuary of his dynasty. He therefore dedicated several altars to the patron saints of the royal family: to Louis, his saintly ancestor, to the memory of his mother, whom he adored, and to the Queen, with the Lady Chapel.

How regrettable it is that all these pictures are mute. Here, where so many cantatas, motets, Te Deums and other glorious holy songs rose to the heavens to celebrate the joys and sorrows of France, all fell silent for ever with the departure of Saint Louis' sons.

Alone, motionless, glittering with gold, King David on the organ screen continues to pluck the strings of his harp, but his song is heard only by God.

"King David playing the harp" after the painting by Domenichino

Gilt bronze Glory by C. Van Cleve below L. Boulogne's celestial concert

The Salon d'Hercule

It was only after the Royal Chapel was completed that the upper part of the adjoining two-storey room — which had been used as the chapel until 1710 — could be converted into a huge salon, where Veronese's great masterpiece, "Christ's meal at the house of Simon", could be displayed.

Robert de Cotte devised the decoration of precious marbles with this painting in mind. But, at that time, the reign of the Sun King was drawing to a close. The era of great construction work was irrevocably over: the war had emptied the royal coffers and Louis XIV's death was imminent. Building was abandoned for twenty years. It was only in 1729 that the young Louis XV ordered de Cotte to complete the task. The décor of marble and bronze is still there today, and the paintings by Veronese have been returned, after more than a century.

The whole setting by de Cotte echoes the background of Veronese's great work. The eye is drawn to the vista glimpsed in the center of the painting, where Mary Magdalen pours perfume over the feet of Jesus. The columns in the painting are repeated on the walls of the room in the form of tall marble pilasters with bronze capitals bearing a gilded cornice. The brilliance of the gold is only equalled here by the marble by Claude Tarlé.

Louis XIV inherited a large collection of masterpieces from his godfather, Cardinal Mazarin. This splendour-loving minister, who was in charge of the King's education, also handed down to him his passion for collecting. The purchase of works of art never ceased right throughout his reign, and, when the monarch died, he left France a considerable inheritance. Louis XIV, then, was an enthusiastic art-lover, but, being the Sun King crowned with a halo of glory and

Bronze relief by Antoine Vassé
(upper section of the
chimneypiece)

youth, he wanted his treasures to be incomparably finer than any in France, and it was not long before his collection had eclipsed those of Charles V and François I.

However, one gap remained in this collection. In this century so enamoured of things Italian, there was not one major work by Paolo Caliari, called Veronese. This deficiency was overcome by diplomacy. Louis XIV's ambassador to the Republic of Venice made known his master's desire to acquire "Christ's meal at the house of Simon", which adorned the convent of the Servites. One obstacle arose: Spain coveted the work in order to offer it to the King of France who did not want to be in her debt in any way. The Republic of Venice settled the matter itself by buying the Veronese and, in a magnificent gesture, offering it to Louis XIV. The latter could only be overjoyed and, on 2nd January 1665, he presented his thanks to the Doge "after having seen this rare and so perfect original". Strangely enough, however, his enthusiasm waned and the painting was relegated to the storerooms of the Louvre. In creating his plans for Versailles, Le Brun never once thought of using it.

In the center bay of the wall nearest to the chapel, another painting by Veronese hangs over a monumental mantelpiece. The upper section of this mantelpiece is adorned with two lion's skins and a head of Hercules. These decorations are in gilt bronze, moulded by Vassé. The painting depicts the meeting of Elizier and Rebecca. Its frame, like that of "Christ's meal at the house of Simon", was carved by Jacques Verberckt.

Louis XV called on the painter François Lemoine to decorate the great ceiling. This artist was still at the beginning of his career when he received the commission which was to establish his dazzling reputation in the eyes of the eighteenth century.

"Hercules"
by Antoine Vassé
(from the mantelpiece)

The
Salon
d'Hercule

32

Ceiling by
François Lemoine
in the
Salon d'Hercule

Lemoine has described his theme for us. "The love of virtue raises man above himself and makes him surmount the most difficult and perilous tasks. Obstacles vanish before the sight of the interests of his King and his country. Sustained by honour and lead by fidelity, he reaches immortality by his actions. The apotheosis of Hercules seemed fitting for the development of my thoughts".

The ceiling is framed by a parapet painted in imitation of white marble; in the corners sit figures symbolizing the virtues of Hercules. The main group is placed in the northern section. Seated amidst the clouds of Olympus, Jupiter, the ruler of the gods, holds the hand of the graceful Hebe who is led by Hymen holding her torch. Hercules, who, through his glorious exploits, has been granted immortality, is represented in a chariot drawn by the spirits of virtue. Lower down, the vices and demons are dragged down towards hell, while the gods and goddesses watch this extraordinary sight impassively.

From the clouds opposite rises the temple of Memory, where Apollo orders a concert to be given by the Muses seated at his feet, not far from Zephyr and Flora "embracing each other tenderly amidst the flowers born of their sighs".

Before leaving the Salon d'Hercule, it should be remembered that Louis XVI had the Deputies of the Estates General presented to him here on 2nd May 1789. A new world was about to dawn... France was turning a page in her history.

The entrance to the State Apartments

"Christ's meal at the house of Simon"
by Veronese

The State Apartments

For Louis XIV, "that monarch who loved grandeur and glory in everything", as Voltaire was to say, the greatest artists, Le Vau, d'Orbay and then Mansart and Le Brun designed a palace whose apartments reached a splendour and wealth previously unheard of. The most extraordinary of all extend to the north of the château's main building and are continued to the west by the magical Hall of Mirrors. Each room was dedicated to a god of antiquity whose planet is one of the sun's satellites.

From 1682, these were the reception apartments. "*Appartement* was the name given to the gathering of the whole Court from seven o'clock in the evening until ten when the King dined. First, there was music, then tables were made ready for all manner of games. Beyond the billiard table was a room set aside for refreshments; and all was perfectly lit..." (Saint-Simon).

The suite
of State
Apartments

The Salon d'Abondance

"Royal Magnificence":
ceiling painted by
René-Antoine Houasse

This room was not considered to be part of the State Apartments until after the North Wing had been built. It was a kind of cul-de-sac which was used as a vestibule for the famous Cabinet des Médailles (now Louis XVI's Games Room) where Louis XIV had gathered together his rarest treasures: paintings, commemorative medals, rock-crystal, *nefs* in gold, and precious stones.

In the center of the ceiling Magnificence appears, "a crown of light around her head, her right hand holding a golden sceptre and the same arm leaning on a cornucopia", as Félibien wrote. Her companions are Immortality and the Fine Arts, symbolized by a figure taking flight and thereby showing the progress made in this field. On either side of the door sit two beautiful women, who may be recognized by their costumes as Europe and Asia.

On the walls covered in velvet or silk, according to the season, the King had hung several masterpieces by Veronese and Poussin, including the former's "Virgin of the Pillar", now in the Louvre. They have now been replaced by portraits of the Sun King's descendants — the Grand Dauphin, his direct heir, who died too soon, and the latter's sons, Philip V of Spain and his brother, the Duc de Bourgogne, who was Louis XV's father. The portrait of Louis XV was painted by J.B. Van Loo, while the others are the work of Hyacinthe Rigaud.

Here, on *Appartement* evenings, buffets were arranged offering hot drinks (coffee and chocolate) or cold (liqueurs, sherbets and fruit juices). In their place now stand several medal-chests in Boulle marquetry, perhaps once part of the splendours of the Cabinet des Médailles. Beside the patinated bronze busts once stood gilded pedestal-tables on which sparkled the crystal candelabra that lit up the drawing-room.

Detail by Houasse
from the ceiling's painted
balustrade

The
Salon
d'Abondance

The Salons of Venus and Diana gave the French an opportunity to draw inspiration from the marble décors that Le Brun had admired during his stay in Italy.

The niche set into the wall of the former Ambassadors' Staircase held, until 1685, the fine statue of Louis XIV in Roman costume, by Jean Warin. Then, until the Revolution, the famous "Mercury tying his sandal" could be seen there. The niche is the center of a majestic setting of marble panels, columns and gilded doors, where painted scenes create for the spectator an illusion of architectural perspectives, all as sham as the statues of Atalanta and Meleager sheltered between the windows.

In the center of the ceiling, Houasse has proclaimed the supremacy of Venus. Stretched out in her chariot, the beautiful goddess receives the crown of roses from the Three Graces. Her son, Cupid, flies above her, while, lower down, the assembly of Olympus, headed by Jupiter, is imprisoned in symbolic garlands testifying to the subjection of the gods and powers to Love.

Here, as in the following rooms, let us imagine on the ceiling a silver chandelier, its lights blending with those of the candelabra on the richly carved and gilded pedestal-tables. Let us dream of two gilded tables between the windows, with alabaster tops adorned with porphyry vases on which the refreshments are laid out: dried fruit, a pyramid of fresh fruit mingled with flowers. The scene is now set for an *Appartement* evening.

"Atalanta": trompe l'œil by J. Rousseau and the doors to the Ambassadors' Staircase

The Salon de Vénus

''The supremacy
of Venus'': ceiling by
René-Antoine Houasse

Here we enter the second room from the great staircase. As for Venus, marble, gold and the beautiful paintings were chosen as fitting for Diana. Apart from the furniture, everything here is original.

When we contemplate these walls, we can sense Le Brun's pleasure as he designed this beautiful geometry of precious marbles in alternating colors.

Blanchard dedicated the center of the ceiling to Apollo's sister, queen of the night, goddess of hunting and fishing, a fierce and sometimes cruel virgin. Diana is seated in her chariot, surrounded by the hours of the night, her daughters. "Sleep and pleasant dreams are at her sides and the nymphs accompanying her prepare the nets".

In the lunettes, Audran and de Lafosse portrayed "the princes who have had the greatest success in navigation or who have been the most dedicated hunters": Cyrus hunting boar, Caesar sending a Roman colony to Carthage, Jason disembarking at Colchos and Alexander hunting lions.

Bronze and marble
in the
Salon de Diane

46

The Salon de Diane

Salon de Diane: ceiling
by G. Blanchard, C. de Lafosse
and C. Audran

47

The room includes two other paintings linked with the story of Diana. We see her painted by Blanchard, "forgetting her pride and her resolution never to love anyone" and going to Endymion. Exactly opposite, above a simple fireplace, de Lafosse presents her coming to rescue Iphigenia. Below this painting, there is a curious little bas-relief by Jacques Sarrazin, "The flight into Egypt". Its presence right in the middle of a completely pagan iconography is quite surprising.

The original noble appearance of this room has been recreated, for during the last few years the pictures have been restored, and the eight classical busts of emperors and empresses returned there. Félibien tells us that "their draperies are of oriental alabaster and their heads are of white marble or porphyry".

But the most famous of all is not among them. It is the one standing against the staircase wall, crowned by two gilt bronze putti, the bust of the young Sun King, carved in white marble with astonishing virtuosity by Gian Lorenzo Bernini during his stay in France in 1665, after having been invited by the King.

A billiard table once stood in the center of the room, "covered with a large carpet of crimson velvet, its edges adorned with a gold fringe". Two platforms would be set up on *Appartement* evenings, "completely covered with a Persian carpet embroidered with gold and silver" and intended for the ladies so that they could look on and applaud more easily the phases of a game at which the King was a past master.

Louis XIV:
bust by
Gian Lorenzo Bernini

Chimneypiece
in the
Salon de Diane

Mars is the god of war and of vengeance. His presence in the King's apartment is therefore a warning to all enemies. The subject-matter of the pictures is ideally suited to what was originally a guard room. Mars Ultor is painted by Audran in the center of the ceiling, preceded by Fame, while Clio writes the book of History. All around, gilded sculptures and paintings continue to relate "the scenes of the heroic actions of the King".

Two paintings have been returned to the walls once adorned with velvet or rich crimson damask — the fine "Louis XV", by Rigaud, and the discreet "Maria Leczinska", by Carl Van Loo, while over the fireplace hangs the celebrated "King David playing the harp", by Domenichino.

One day we hope to celebrate the return of the "Tent of Darius" by Le Brun and the "Pilgrims of Emmaeus", by Veronese, which were the pride of this room.

Four Titians, now in the Louvre, once hung over the doors and in their place are allegories by Simon Vouet commissioned for the château at Saint-Germain.

Between the three windows, as Félibien tells us, are "two large crystal mirrors; and beneath the mirrors we see chalcedony tables with rock crystal candelabra on either side, standing on gilded pedestal-tables".

Other candelabra, two beautiful tables made for the Duc d'Antin and several magnificent Gobelins tapestries make up the present decoration of this remarkable salon.

Louis XV
in coronation robes,
by Hyacinthe Rigaud

The Salon de Mars

The ceiling: center by C. Audran,
and roundels by C. Audran,
J. Jouvenet and R.-A. Houasse

The newspaper "Mercure Galant" gives us the key to the superb ceiling of this great salon which was the Sun King's first large state bedchamber at Versailles. Mercury "appears in the centre of the ceiling (by J-B de Champaigne) in a chariot drawn by cocks; Vigilance, Care, Agility, Science, Industry and Music follow or precede him. Four large paintings accompany this central piece and portray Princes having conquered their enemies by dexterity and who, through their industry, have earned immortal glory".

Vigilance may be recognized by her symbolic bird, the crane, with its wings spread. The subjects of the coves are, starting from the left, "The reception given by Alexander for an Indian embassy", then "Ptolemy in discussion with scholars in his library", the best known of all, that of Alexandria, a fitting allusion "to mark the magnificence of the Royal Library". Then follows "Augustus receiving an Indian embassy", and "Alexander and Aristotle", the latter receiving from this prince various

The threshold
of the Salon
de Mercure

The Salon de Mercure

"Mercury triumphant":
ceiling by
Jean-Baptiste de Champaigne

foreign animals whose description he is to write, an allusion to the celebrated menagerie built on the banks of the Grand Canal and destroyed during the Revolution.

The Salon de Mercure, like that of Apollo which follows, evokes a curious atmosphere of nostalgia filled with regret. It was once a setting of extraordinary splendour and the finest taste. The automaton clock made by Antoine Morand in 1706 for the elderly Louis XIV still chimes the notes of a gay carillon when Apollo reaches his Zenith in the heavens; the richly ornamentated commodes made by André Charles Boulle in 1708 for the King's bedchamber at Trianon are also here; but these pieces are the only survivors preserved at Versailles from the collection amassed by Louis XIV — the rest has been lost or scattered.

The greatest loss must surely be that of the fabulous silver furniture which was the glory of France for almost a decade: the long, solid silver balustrade with its eight candelabra, the pedestals, the vases, the great chandelier and the mirror with its finely chased frame. Gone too are the extremely rich gold and silver embroidery hangings that covered the walls, and the gold-edged silks on which were hung masterpieces such as the "Deposition" and the "Pilgrims of Emmaeus" by Titian, or the "Holy Family" and "Saint Michael" by Raphael.

After he had been declared King of Spain, the Duc d'Anjou slept in this room under the protection of the messenger of the gods from 16th November to 4th December 1700. When his grandfather, the Sun King, died, his body was displayed here for a week, watched over by seventy-two priests celebrating Mass in continuous relays. The same ceremony took place in 1774 on the death of Louis XV.

The Spanish defeat
at the Bruges canal
(detail from a tapestry)

The clock
by Antoine Morand
in the Salon de Mercure

For a King born under the sign of fire, Le Brun designed a throne-room dedicated to one of the great deities of Olympus, Apollo, the patron of the arts, the symbol of the sun and civilizing light.

On the ceiling, in a frame carried by frail nymphs, the god himself appears. It is dawn, Apollo rises from the waves in his chariot drawn by four steeds and leaps into his race around the earth. Flora, Ceres, Bacchus and Saturn, who symbolize the seasons, accompany him, while France and Magnificence are awakened by the sound of this wondrous event. In the coves, Charles de Lafosse also created paintings alluding to the reign of Louis XIV — Coriolanus raising the siege of Rome, Vespasian ordering the Coliseum to be built, Augustus constructing the port of Mysene and Porus brought before Alexander. The figures in the corners represent the four parts of the earth.

The walls once had as their pride the set of paintings by Guido Reni dedicated to the Hercules myth. Over the marble fireplace, in summer, hung the famous portrait of the King in coronation robes, painted by Rigaud. At the end of the room, on a dais covered with a Savonnerie carpet, stood the silver throne under a canopy hung with rich curtains. The official audiences took place in this room but, on *Appartement* evenings, Louis XIV would sit in relaxed fashion on the edge of the platform, giving orders to the musicians. Gobelins tapestries from the History of the King series and a carpet with solar motifs constitute the present décor.

The central panel
of the doors in the
Salon d'Apollon

The Salon d'Apollon

Ceiling of the
Salon d'Apollon by
Charles de Lafosse

59

The splendours of the State Apartments seem to have been designed only to announce the even more astounding ones of the Hall of Mirrors and the two salons on either side of it. Mansart's construction of the Salon de la Guerre, which was begun in 1679, and then of the Hall of Mirrors and the Salon de la Paix, involved the destruction of three rooms in the King's Apartments, beyond the Salon d'Apollon.

Here as in the Hall of Mirrors, Le Brun created an immortal masterpiece. He worked from 1683 to 1701 with a team of painters, sculptors and plasterers. Piganiol de la Force describes his intentions for us: "As this room is dedicated to Bellona, the ornamentation of the frieze consists entirely of war trophies, thunderbolts and shields. Over the doors are large, gilt metal trophies. Below are the four seasons portrayed by masks and signifying that Louis the Great is their conqueror". Unfortunately, the battles of mankind are far more lethal than these, as the ceiling shows.

"Winter",
over the
mirror-doors

The Salon de la Guerre

"France at war":
ceiling by
Charles Le Brun

In the center of the domed ceiling, France, helmeted and brandishing a thunderbolt against her enemies, protects herself with a shield bearing Louis XIV's portrait. She is surrounded by a circle of Victories holding paintings and standards commemorating battles. The cove paintings proclaim the confusion of the vanquished: Holland; Germany kneeling and covering herself with her shield; Spain in a last desperate attempt seizing a pike, while her lion rises up with a roar. All these war scenes have great dramatic beauty.

These gory themes gave one of our greatest sculptors the opportunity to create a masterpiece in which war is glorified through the triumph and splendour of the victor. Between the door of the Salon d'Apollon and a false door concealed by mirrors, over the fireplace flanked by two slaves bound with flowers, Coysevox modelled in stucco the glorious image of Louis XIV Imperator galloping to victory. At the top of the frame, the trumpets of Fame accompany the hero, whose exploits Clio, sitting calmly in the hearth, writes in the book of History.

Of the four busts with porphyry heads and bronze drapery, only two have been returned. A large chandelier with azure-colored crystals has replaced the gilded pedestal-tables holding candelabra. In Louis XIV's time the six long curtains were of white damask with his monogram embroidered in gold. These and Louis XV's green satin ones, have gone. Nevertheless, the essence of the room lies in the marvellous décor, and this remains to fire the imagination.

A trophy in bronze relief

Relief sculpture by
Antoine Coysevox
in the Salon de la Guerre

The Hall of Mirrors

« *Sur le céleste plan des voûtes azurées,*
Les miennes furent mesurées,
Par les plus grands Maîtres des Arts :
Les beautez de mon ciel attirent les regards,
Mansart dans son Architecture,
Comme Lebrun par sa Peinture,
Ont signalé de toutes parts
Le talent qu'ils avaient d'imiter la nature »
(Monicart)

The plan for the Hall of Mirrors was approved by the King on 26th September 1678, and work was begun immediately. Together with its two salons, it extends along the whole west façade of the château. It is two hundred and forty feet long, thirty-three feet wide and its incomparable ceiling towers to a height of forty feet.

Through seventeen high arched windows light pours in onto the mirrors opposite. Down both sides, the arches are divided by twenty-four red marble pilasters with gilt bronze bases. Their gilded Corinthian and French-style capitals with fleur-de-lis and cocks are the work of Philippe Caffiéri. Between each bay of three openings, emphasising the triple rhythm of the Hall, are broad piers adorned with rich trophies in bronze relief and flanked by pilasters, or, in the central section of the Hall, marble niches containing classical statues. At either end, a wide arch opens into the Salons de la Guerre and de la Paix.

Antique statue:
the "Versailles
Bacchus"

Lamp bearers
in the
Hall of Mirrors

Around the top runs a cornice on double modillions and scrolls, and above it sits a series of enchanting sculptures of trophies supported by cherubs, the work of a whole team of excellent artists (Coysevox, Leconte, Massou, Le Gros, Flamen). Over all is the celebrated ceiling, painted by Le Brun, to which we shall return a little later.

Originally the hall had solid silver furniture, ordered by Louis XIV, designed by Le Brun and made by the finest silversmiths. It formed part of the country's monetary reserves, which had been converted into works of art.

"There were tables of such marvellous sculpture and engraving that the heavy solid silver constituted scarcely one tenth of their value".

Amidst this dazzling pomp, Louis XIV and his successor granted memorable audiences to the ambassadors of the most far-flung countries, Persia, Siam, Turkey. They also held balls or games here for their courtiers on the occasion of marriages in the royal family. For such celebrations, the light from the gilt candlestands was strengthened by three rows of crystal chandeliers hanging from the ceiling; in addition, there were stools with carved legs, numerous curtains and, on the floor, forty vases in marble, porphyry and alabaster. The Venus of Arles, Diana with a hind and the so-called Germanicus by Cleomenes decorated the niches in the company of other classical statues which were returned here a short time ago. However, the really important feature has survived intact: the long ceiling by Le Brun, a gigantic pictorial poem dedicated to the glory of Louis XIV. The center illustrates the year 1661, when Mazarin died and the young King decided to govern by himself, without a prime minister, to the astonishment of France's neighbouring powers. On either side, a series of smaller panels, scenes *en grisaille* and symbolical figures proclaim the grandeur of the first seventeen years of this personal reign. It is one of the largest pictorial compositions in the western world.

After the departure of its Kings and the Revolution, the Hall fell into a deep slumber, from which it was woken on 3rd January 1805 by the arrival of an august visitor, Pope Pius VII. In pontifical robes and tiara, he moved towards the central balcony to bless the crowd which had invaded the whole garden. Then, silence fell once more, broken from time to time by the appearance of illustrious visitors, such as Queen Victoria of England in 1855, until a deadly thunderbolt struck at the heart of France's national pride: on 18th January 1871, after the defeat of Napoleon III, Bismarck, the chancellor of Prussia, chose this important spot, the symbol of France's power and prestige, to have his sovereign, William I, recognized as emperor of Germany. For this reason, France and the Allied Powers chose the Hall of Mirrors forty years later for the ceremony ratifying the Treaty of Versailles which, on 28th June 1919, put an end to the First World War and led the world into a new era, the twentieth century.

Charles Le Brun: "Crossing the Rhine in the presence of the enemy" (detail from the ceiling)

PASSAGE DV RHIN

Originally created at the same time as the Salon de la Guerre, this room retained its present appearance only briefly, for it was assigned by Louis XIV to the Queen and to the Dauphines and, in 1729, was separated from the Hall of Mirrors by a painted screen which could be removed in half-an-hour on the occasion of great ceremonies.

The center of the ceiling is again dedicated to the supremacy of France. Crowned by Glory, with a shield in one hand and a sceptre in the other, she crosses the skies in a chariot drawn by four doves and bearing the arms of the Dauphines of France and of the Queen of Spain, the Sun King's niece. Around the chariot are Peace holding her caduceus, Hymen holding her torch and crowned by the Three Graces, and Abundance with her cornucopia. Finally Le Brun has painted the sovereign Authority, Religion together with Innocence and masked Heresy, and Magnificence, seated upon riches, showing France the plans of buildings.

An overdoor
from the Salon
de la Paix

The Salon de la Paix

Ceiling by Charles Le Brun:
"Apotheosis
of France"

In the paintings on the lunettes, little winged cherubs fly to Holland, Spain and Germany who are enjoying the benefits of peace; Christian Europe, holding the pontifical tiara in one hand and a cornucopia in the other, cannot help rejoicing at such a peaceful sight.

The decoration of the walls echoes that of the Salon de la Guerre, with marble panels, gilded trophies and false mirror doors sparkling in the midday light. The large oval painting by François Lemoine, depicting Louis XV bestowing peace on Europe, was hung above the fireplace in July 1729. The King stands upright, trampling on the allegory of luxury and holding out an olive branch to Europe. Behind rises the temple of Janus, with Discord trying to open its doors; to prevent her, Minerva, seated on a cloud, gives her orders to Mercury, the symbol of negotiation. On the right, Piety presents to Europe the King's twin eldest daughters, the babies Elisabeth and Henriette, whom Fecundity holds in her arms. In the foreground of the painting sit the genii of the Arts and Trade, the children of Peace.

On becoming the Queen's Games Room for Maria Leczinska, consort to Louis XV, this room received a new suite of furniture, composed essentially of forty stools for the players who were seated around small games tables. Later, Marie-Antoinette ordered a chest-of-drawers and two rosewood corner-cupboards. Two very fine pieces of this Queen's furnishings have remained here — the gilt bronze andirons in the shape of lions, sculpted by Thomire in 1786, which adorn the fireplace. We should also remember that, for almost forty years, Maria Leczinska held here each Sunday one of her famous concerts of sacred or secular music, given before elegant and cultured audiences.

François Lemoine:
"Louis XV bestowing
peace on Europe" (detail)

The
Salon
de la Paix

The entrance
to the King's
Apartments

The King's Apartments

In his plans for enlarging Versailles, Le Vau had decided that the State Apartments would be the King's apartments. This indeed was the case until 1682, when Louis XIV moved to the wings overlooking the Marble Courtyard, into the large suite which was used by Louis XV and Louis XVI for their official functions. It consists of five rooms which are reached by the Queen's Staircase: the Guard Room, the first and second antechamber (called the Salon de l'Œil de Bœuf), the Bedchamber and, finally, the Council Chamber. The first two rooms suffered badly during the nineteenth century when, in an attempt to "improve" their appearance, they were covered in a thick coat of distemper in imitation marble.

The Queen's Staircase therefore also became the King's Staircase from 1682. Built between 1679 and 1681 after the completion, on the other side of the Royal Courtyard, of the Ambassadors' Staircase, it was enlarged in 1701 by the addition of a loggia leading to the apartments of the King and, opposite, to those of Madame de Maintenon.

How many famous men climbed this superb stairway. It still resounds with the steps of Louvois, Saint-Simon, Mansart and so many others on their way, each morning and evening, to attend the rising and retiring of the King.

The loggia
of the Queen's
Staircase

The Salon de l'Œil de Bœuf

The Bull's Eye Room was created in 1701. However, it was not given its strange name until the reign of Louis XV who enjoyed making fun of the oval window in the cornice. Its walls are lined with carved wood-panelling alternating with large mirrors and paintings. At the attic level, a frieze on a white background "embellished with roses and a trellis like a network of gold" depicts children at play, a lively subject portrayed with great freshness of imagination.

As this room led to the royal bedchamber, it was assigned a very special rôle. For the princes and lords admitted to the King's Rising Ceremony, this was the perfect meeting place to hear of the sovereign's decisions and Court events. For one had to wait a long time before being admitted to the bedchamber. First came the "family entrance" reserved for the Children of France and Princes of the Blood. This corresponded to the "Private Rising Ceremony" which took place after the departure of the doctor, the surgeon and the King's old nurse who came to kiss him each morning until 1688. Then followed the "state entrance" for the high dignitaries of the crown, the "first entrance" for those who had the privilege of a "royal warrant" and, finally, the "chamber entrance" for those admitted to the "State Rising Ceremony". These last had to wait more than an hour since the door would close after each person and its two halves were opened only for the Grand Dauphin and Princes of the Blood.

Louis XIV and his family,
by Jean Nocret,
in the Bull's Eye Room

"This drawing-room
precedes
the royal bedchamber"

The King's Bedchamber

The whole of Versailles radiated out from the bedchamber of Louis XIV which is its geometrical center. This is the meeting- and starting-point of the axes along which Le Vau, Mansart and Le Nôtre aligned the palaces, avenues and lakes. Each morning, in this universe dedicated to the cult of Apollo, the first rays of light struck the windows of the room where the Sun King slept. It was an old tradition in France that the royal bedchamber should be the center of the palace. As we have seen, it was not until 1701 that this custom was put into practice at Versailles.

After the first large-scale construction work by Le Vau in 1668, this room was named the "Grand Salon". At that time it was lit not only by the three windows to the east, but also by three to the west, which led to the terrace later filled by the Hall of Mirrors. Lying between the King's Apartment and those of the Queen, the "Grand Salon" filled the role later played by the Hall of Mirrors. Its décor, altered when the latter was built in 1679, was left intact from then on; the great white ceiling, the gilded panelling broken by sixteen tall pilasters flanking the doors, windows and mirrors, all date from that time.

During this same period, the façade overlooking the Marble Courtyard was altered and embellished; the rectangular windows were arched and opened onto a gilded balcony supported by eight marble columns, and the whole façade was crowned with stone carvings of the figures of Mars and Hercules.

"France watching over the King
in his slumber"
(Photograph lent by R.M.N.).

The bedchamber
seen from
the royal alcove

The year 1701 saw large-scale construction work on all the King's apartments, and it was then that the Grand Salon became the King's Bedchamber. The three blocked French windows on the west were removed to make way for a large inset archway forming the alcove. In the center, above the cornice, the King ordered the creation of a "richly ornamented mosaic ground, in the middle of which a beautiful figure representing France would be seated on trophies beneath a rich canopy attached at the top of the arch and held at the corners by two genii, and for the corners of the ceiling above the arch to be adorned with two figures of Fame". This statue of France above the bed, watching over her King in his slumber, was to be the work of Nicolas Coustou.

Another of the most important architectural elements is the balustrade which has been miraculously preserved. It is there to protect the royal bed, in the same way as it protects the altar in a chapel and delineates the limit beyond which one may not pass. "L'état de la France" of 1708 tells us that "a valet remains seated on the inside of the balustrade to guard the bed, and at meal times one of his fellow valets takes his place. This valet must guard the bed and prevent anyone within the enclosure from approaching it... The ushers keep their eyes open for anyone who might put his hat on, comb his hair or sit down in the chamber, on the seats, on a table or on the balustrade of the alcove... When the King leaves the château of Versailles for a few days, a valet remains there to guard the bed, and sleeps at the foot of His Majesty's bed".

The bed, then, symbolized the sanctuary of royalty, and it was of the utmost splendour. Félibien gives us several details which are completed by other visitors of the time, and corroborated by the precious archives of the former "Crown Furniture Repository". The walls of the alcove and the bed were hung with the same type of fabric, altered according to the seasons; the bed, as Félibien describes, "is hung with crimson velvet so richly covered with gold embroidery that the background can hardly be made out". The velvet was intended to warm the room in autumn and winter and, at these periods only, two paintings were hung on either side of the bed, the "David" by Domenichino, which is now in the Salon de Mars, and a "Saint John", attributed at the time to Raphael.

The furnishings were completed by door-curtains to protect the entrances, twelve folding-stools, two armchairs in the alcove and crimson curtains for the three large windows overlooking the Marble Courtyard.

The brocade or velvet hangings were particularly sumptuous. The best known of all is undoubtedly the one delivered by Lallié for the winter of 1701 — a crimson velvet, superbly embroidered with gold thread, which Louis XVI, unable to have restored because it was worn, ordered to be burnt to retrieve the precious metal. This wall-hanging was changed at the coming of spring when the embroidered velvet made way for the richest of brocades from Lyons, woven from several hundred grams of gold.

The exceptional nature of this room, the sanctuary of royalty, where the monarch who had raised his country to the heights of glory, fortune and artistic achievement passed away on the morning of 1st September 1715, after having reigned over France for seventy-two years, inspired all those who have been in charge of Versailles to restore the room as completely as possible. After long years of effort the décor of this bedchamber has been totally reconstituted.

The wood-panelling here today was entirely removed and repaired. The carved ornamentation stands out vividly from the white background, its elegance enhanced by the glittering gold. The light streaming in from the attic storey and the three large windows brings out the harmony of the sculpted decoration while its sumptuous impact is softened by the grace of childhood and youth evoked by eight young figures above the doors and the smiling putti leaning on their elbows in the mirror frames above the two fireplaces.

The pictorial décor, consisting of the fine paintings of the evangelists by Valentin de Boulogne and Lanfranco's "Agar in the Desert", has been returned to the attic storey.

For the newly-woven fabrics, a summer wall-hanging was chosen from fragments of the original. Thanks to many generous private donations, the silk-weavers of Lyons wove a masterpiece for the alcove wall and the bed : a crimson silk superbly embroidered with gold and silver thread. This fabric, which also covers the chairs and folding-stools, restores to this room, for visitors to admire, its dazzling luxury of yesteryear.

Saint Matthew,
by Valentin de Boulogne
(Photograph lent by R.M.N.).

The
King's
Bedchamber

As we turn the page, we enter the Council Chamber and thus leave the grandeur of the Sun King for the grace and elegance of Louis XV. In 1755, Gabriel united into one vast room the two smaller ones that were previously here: Louis XIV's Council Chamber, and the room called the Cabinet des Termes (or of periwigs).

Gabriel brought life to these walls by the interplay of solids (doors or panelling) and empty spaces (windows or mirrors), charming to behold. He himself designed the carved panels in which Antoine Rousseau has presented us with a masterpiece. The most admirable are those on either side of the fireplace, with bold, handsome frames and, in the center of each, a pendant cartouche of *putti* "playing at the King's council" within sprays of leaves.

Around the covered table which was set up on council days, the ministers sat on folding-stools, while the King presided from an armchair. The passing of time was shown by the clock on the mantelpiece, next to which, on a velvet cushion, slept Louis XV's large angora cat.

The bust of Alexander the Great, with its gilt bronze drapery, and that of Scipio Africanus stood here in the eighteenth century. They have recently been returned to Versailles, as have the two vases of Mars and Minerva, commissioned by Louis XVI for the mantelpiece.

The King's Council Chamber

Jules-Antoine Rousseau:
details of the carved
panelling

As it lay beyond the bedchamber, access to the King's Council Chamber was extremely difficult for the courtiers. It was entered by ministers on council days. There, for almost a century, important decisions involving the destiny of France and Europe were taken. In the evenings, the King sometimes invited the members of his family there. At times, after his rising ceremony, he would have one of the lords who had asked him for an audience called into this room. The lucky person chosen remained standing to announce his request; the conversation was therefore brief, but it nevertheless aroused the curiosity and jealousy of the crowd of courtiers who had remained in the chamber. It was in this room that, according to Etiquette, the King received ladies who had been accepted as residents at Court.

The Court also passed through this room to pay homage to the sovereign on the occasion of marriages in the royal family or, after a death, dressed in long mourning robes, to offer its condolences.

Alexander the Great in marble, porphyry and gilt bronze by François Girardon

87

The King's
Council
Chamber

89

This suite, which was created by Louis Le Vau for Queen Marie-Thérèse, consists of four large rooms whose windows open onto the Parterre du Midi, with its beautiful embroidery of brightly colored flowers.

It is reached by means of the famous Queen's Staircase with its extremely rich decoration. The balustrade is of black marble with red balusters. "A large array of Ionic pilasters" of Dinan marble adorns the upper storey, where cherubs and sphinxes of gilt metal decorate the overdoors. These bas-reliefs are the work of Le Gros and Massou who also created the charming trophy in the niche on the landing representing two cherubs holding an escutcheon with the royal arms crowned by two doves.

On the wall opposite the loggia, a trompe-l'œil painting of architecture adds a pleasant note while increasing the sense of space.

It was customary for this suite of rooms, where the royal line was perpetuated, to remain in continual use. Thus it was lived in by Queen Marie-Thérèse (1682-1683), the Dauphine of Bavaria (1683-1690), the Dauphine of Savoy (Louis XV's mother) (1690-1712), the Spanish Infanta (Louis XV's fiancée) (1722-1725), Queen Maria Leczinska (1725-1768) and Marie-Antoinette as Dauphine and then as Queen (1770-1789).

The Queen's Apartment

A trophy with
doves and royal monogram
by P. Le Gros and B. Massou

Room of the Queen's Guard

With its marble and paintings, which come from the former Jupiter Cabinet (the King's first Council Chamber on the site of the Salon de la Guerre), the Room of the Queen's Guard is one of the finest achievements of Le Brun's art. The white and red marble inlays are strikingly enhanced by bold frames of black marble around both real and false doors, paintings and chimney-piece. Fine gilt-metal bas-reliefs and a Languedoc marble fireplace complete the effect of grandeur.

On the octagonal ceiling Noël Coypel painted the ruler of the gods, Jupiter. He stands upright in a silver chariot drawn by two eagles. Around him hover four children, symbolizing satellites of this god's planet which itself appears beneath the chariot in the form of a woman.

Justice and Piety accompany Jupiter. Justice is armed with an axe to punish the vices, while Piety strews the contents of a cornucopia as a reward for the virtues. Félibien tells us that in the coves the painter portrayed, in four large paintings, "two of Justice's most memorable actions, and two of Piety's most renowned deeds, whose memory has been preserved by History and which have a particular connection with several of the many examples of these virtues given by the King". These examples are "Ptolemy Philadelphia freeing the Jews",

Bas-relief
in gilt metal
by P. Le Gros and B. Massou

"Jupiter, accompanied by
Justice and Piety":
ceiling by Noël Coypel

93

"Alexander Severus having corn distributed to the people during a time of famine", "Trajan dispensing justice", and "Solon explaining his laws". Coypel is also the creator of the two paintings, the "Sacrifice to Jupiter", above the fireplace, and, opposite, the "Dance of the Corybants".

Night and day the Queen's guards would keep watch. The room was continually cluttered with racks for their arms and particularly with screens hiding tables and camp-beds.

The usefulness of a room of this kind, strategically placed at the entrance to the Queen's Apartment, was tragically demonstrated by the events of 6th October 1789, on an evening when a mob seething with excitement tried to force the doors which protected what was to be the Queen's last night at Versailles. The fight was a bloody one, but the devotion of the guards enabled the Queen to slip away and seek refuge with the King and also gave the National Guard time to arrive as reinforcements.

"Dance
of the Corybants"
by Noël Coypel

Room of the Queen's Guard:
"Sacrifice to Jupiter"
by Noël Coypel

95

This vast room, abundantly lit by three large windows, forms, to the south, the symmetrical counterpart to the Salon de Mars in the State Apartments to the north. The effect of time on Le Brun's decoration has often been disastrous. The central ceiling painting, in which Vignon had portrayed the god Mars, has gone and a more peaceful subject, "Darius' Tent", by Le Brun, has taken its place. All the rest of the ceiling, with its battle scenes in gold monochrome, has fortunately remained, as have the fine military trophies with *putti* bearing eagles in the corners of the ceiling coves.

The nineteenth century continued the work of destruction. Two of the large carved doors were removed at the same time as the mantelpiece and its mirror.

And at this time, the last traces of the gallery for

The "Grand Couvert" Antechamber

"Queen Marie-Antoinette
and her children"
by Elizabeth-Louise Vigée-Lebrun

96

Marie-Antoinette's musicians, which occupied the wall of the adjoining Guard Room, were also removed. The tapestries chosen by Marie-Antoinette are still in existence and this room may one day be restored to its former glory.

From the time of Louis XIV, the King's "Grand Couvert" was held in this room. Armchairs for the King and Queen were placed in front of the fireplace, together with a table set for two. The Marquise de la Tour du Pin describes, in her memoirs, a "grand couvert" at which she was present in 1788 : "The Queen sat on the left of the King (Louis XVI and Marie-Antoinette). Their backs were to the fireplace and, ten feet in front of them, arranged in a semi-circle, were a number of stools on which were seated the duchesses, princesses or those in high office who held this privilege... (behind them stood the other people present). The King ate with a hearty appetite, but the Queen did not remove her gloves nor use her serviette, which was a great error". By this remark, the narrator tells us that Marie-Antoinette, who had been accustomed to the informality of life at the Austrian Court, never got used to this practice of the "grand couvert", which, Madame Campan assures us, was "the joy of the provincial visitors and good people" admitted to watch the King and Queen dine at Versailles.

War
trophy
(ceiling corner)

This room could be considered as the Queen's official drawing-room. Here, surrounded by her ladies-in-waiting, she had presented to her the ladies of the nobility who had recently been admitted to reside at Court. For important official ceremonies, for instance when an ambassador and his wife came to pay their respects, her chair was placed against the far wall on a dais under a canopy.

Of the setting designed by Le Brun, we can still admire the fine ceiling by Michel Corneille dedicated to Mercury. In the round central section, the god hovers over our heads, spreading his influence over the arts and sciences. He is accompanied by Eloquence, Poetry, Geometry etc. Félibien explains that other allegorical figures in this painting represent "Learning and Vigilance, without which one can make no progress in the sciences or the arts". On the ceiling coves, held up as an example to women of the time, we see Sappho playing the lyre, Penelope weaving tapestry, Aspasia with the Greek philosophers and Ceriseme painting, which, with music, was Maria Leczinska's favourite pastime.

The walls were originally lined with panels of richest marble, probably somewhat like those in the Salon de Diane. However this material was most inconvenient in winter in a room so difficult to heat. It was therefore partly covered with tapestries. Several chests-of-drawers with inlaid flowers, a fine crystal chandelier and a number of stools completed this set of furnishings which lasted until 1785. In that year, Marie-Antoinette, who did not appreciate the nobility of Louis XIV's décor, decided to have the marble removed and kept only the painted ceiling.

It was then that the white and gold dado wood-panelling was created and the

The camel clock
and the
ostrich candelabra

The Salon des Nobles

"Mercury spreading his influence
over the Arts and Sciences":
ceiling by Michel Corneille

walls were hung with apple-green silk framed with a galloon of gold thread. A very fine slate-blue mantelpiece, decorated with bronzes by Gouthière, was then placed beneath one of the three large mirrors. Louis-Philippe had this removed, but it has been found again and replaced in position.

Some items of Marie-Antoinette's furniture have also been found: two corner-cupboards and two of the three magnificent mahogany commodes made by Riesener in 1786. Since then, the donation of an admirable rock crystal chandelier and the arrival of the spectacular "camel" clock and the "ostrich" candelabra have added an exceptional touch of luxury to this room.

When the occupant of this room died, it was the custom for the body to be placed on view here. A most painful event occurred in 1712, when the coffins of Louis XV's parents were displayed in the Salon, after they had been struck down in the prime of youth within days of each other.

The Salon
des Nobles
de la Reine

The Queen's Bedchamber

Here is one of the finest and most appealing masterpieces that the decorative arts have offered France. The removal of Le Brun's décor should cause no regret. The one designed by de Cotte and Gabriel and his son for Maria Leczinska is matchless. Under the most beautiful gilded sky in which François Boucher painted the Queen's virtues (Charity, Abundance, Fidelity and Prudence), Dugoulon, Le Goupil and Verberckt created elegant panelling with rococo ornamentation around three large, sparkling mirrors that were framed by gilded palm trees.

Furnishings of particular richness were required for this setting. Some of the finest fabrics made in Lyons in the eighteenth century were chosen for the alcove, the most sumptuous of all being those given to his wife by Louis XV.

Marie-Antoinette asked for some alterations to be made and the corners of the ceiling were therefore adorned with trophies in which the arms of France and Navarre alternate with those of the House of Austria. She had the portraits of Maria Leczinska's parents over the mirrors replaced by tapestry portraits of her mother, Maria Theresa, her brother, Joseph II, and her husband. Finally, in 1786, the large modern fireplace of red marble was installed; recently the andirons in the shape of sphinxes have been returned to stand guard in the hearth.

After the last world war, the only piece of this room's furniture which remained at Versailles was the screen by Sené and the sumptuous jewellery-cabinet delivered by Evalde and Schwerdfeger in 1787. It was not a great deal. However, samples of the fabric which hung in the alcove in October 1789 had been preserved at Lyons and, in addition, we were fortunate enough to be able to purchase the Queen's original bedspread in New York, in 1955. It was then decided to reconstruct all the missing material. Thanks to watercolors which were found and documents in the archives, it became possible to recreate meticulously the carvings on the missing bedhead and canopy. A new balustrade was also carved. The large Savonnerie carpet had just been donated to Versailles, and the one inside the alcove was rewoven at the Savonnerie works from the half still in existence.

No less than twenty years of unceasing effort were required to conclude this restoration work which was made possible only through the generosity of many patrons and the talent of the artisans who are the heirs of the eighteenth century masters.

Among the memories one could evoke here are the moments of joy at the birth of the nineteen Children of France. Tradition had it that these births should

Décor by R. de Cotte
and the Gabriels for
the Queen's alcove

Restored
since
June 1975

103

be public so that the legitimacy of the children could not be questioned. Madame Campan tells of the birth of Madame Royale, the first child born to Louis XVI and Marie-Antoinette.

"Madame, the King's daughter, came into the world before noon on 19th December 1778. The etiquette permitting the indiscriminate entry of all present for the confinement of the Queens was observed to such an exaggerated degree that, when the accoucheur announced in a loud voice, "The Queen is about to give birth", the mass of curious onlookers who surged into the room was so huge and so tumultuous that it was thought this movement would kill the Queen".

The last anecdote connected with this room is a dramatic one. It was here that Marie-Antoinette spent her last night at Versailles, interrupted at dawn on 6th October 1789 by the mob which had arrived from Paris the night before and which tried unsuccessfully to force the entrances to her apartment.

"The Virtues of the Queen":
ceiling panels painted
by François Boucher

The arms of France,
Navarre and Austria at
the ceiling corners

107

The Queen's Private Suite

The only private realm of the Queen of France at Versailles, this set of small drawing-rooms opening onto rather dark interior courtyards bears witness to each sovereign's desire for a life of her own. They were created at the time of Louis XIV for Marie-Thérèse and were extended little by little with each reign.

For more than four decades, the discreet Maria Leczinska loved to take refuge here, to flee from the intrigues and bitterness of her existence. She would spend many long hours here in the company of friends, talking, doing embroidery and painting under the direction of J.B. Oudry. She gave these rooms a graceful, personal touch by adorning them with magnificent rococo wainscoting and paintings by Boucher and Nattier.

Nothing remains today of these delightful creations of Louis XV's reign...

Portrait of
Maria Leczinska
by Jean-Marc Nattier

The Cabinet Doré
designed by
Richard Mique

The Cabinet
de la
Méridienne

From 1770 a breath of youth and new life swept through Versailles. The Dauphin, the future Louis XVI, had just married the archduchess Marie-Antoinette. The dynamic princess, who had seen only fourteen springs, wanted everything about her to be modern. Her royal spouse, deeply in love with her, could refuse her nothing and had everything redecorated by Richard Mique, who became the Queen's architect.

Being of secondary importance, the bathroom and retiring room were hardly altered, so that it was possible to put back the magnificent paintings by J.-B. Oudry depicting the five senses, commissioned by Maria Leczinska. Mique's masterpiece at the palace of Versailles is definitely the Cabinet Doré, where the superb wood-panelling, carved in 1783 by the Rousseau brothers, is adorned with sphinxes, incense-burners and arabesques, alternating with mirror-panels. In this sumptuous setting, Marie-Antoinette would welcome her friends who were often mischievous and given to mockery; here she would train her pretty voice to sing under the direction of Grétry, or pose for Madame Vigée-Lebrun.

Beyond is the new library and, lastly, the charming Cabinet de la Méridienne, given by Louis XVI to his wife in 1781 on the occasion of the birth of the Dauphin.

This room, situated behind the alcove of the Queen's bedchamber, is enchantingly decorated with sparkling mirrors reflecting the exquisitely gilded panelling and the blue damask rewoven for the window, alcove and chairs.

The
Queen's Private
Suite

111

The King's Private Suite

This series of drawing-rooms extends along the first floor of the château and is lit from both the Marble Courtyard and the Royal Courtyard. Louis XIV had gathered in these rooms the rarest masterpieces in his collection of paintings as well as all kinds of objets d'art — bronzes, medals and rock crystal.

Louis XV considered this decoration uncomfortable and, in 1738, ordered his architect, Gabriel, to transform the whole apartment. Work continued until the end of his reign and, in 1774, Louis XVI created a new masterpiece — his library.

Some of the splendid pieces of furniture commissioned by Louis XV and Louis XVI for these rooms, scattered during the Revolution, have been returned to their original places during the last twenty years and are offered for the admiration of all visitors to Versailles.

Portrait on glass
of Louis XV in 1774
by Vincent de Monpetit

The barometer with case by
Lemaire in the foreground;
beyond, the Antechamber of the Dogs

The King's Suite was reached from the ground-floor of the Royal Courtyard through a guard room which was partly destroyed during the last century. From there one took the staircase called the King's Steps and entered via the Antechamber of the Dogs.

This room, where the kennels of Louis XV's little dogs stood, opened on one side onto the After-Hunt Dining-Room, created by Gabriel in 1750, and, on the other, onto the Clock Cabinet. From the antechamber one enters the bedchamber arranged for Louis XV in 1738 on the site of Louis XIV's former billiards room.

During the sixteen years following his return to Versailles, Louis XV had slept each night in Louis XIV's bedchamber. He finally decided to leave this noble room in 1738 because, despite all the improvements made, it remained icy in winter.

For the new bedchamber, Gabriel chose a room facing south which he covered in pier-glasses and carved panelling still there today. The bed was placed in an alcove originally flanked by large carved palm-trees and closed off by a balustrade which disappeared during the Revolution. This room was undoubtedly one of the most dazzling at Versailles during the eighteenth century. Today, to restore some life to it, a tapestry bedspread made in 1740 has replaced the royal bedspread, without, however, attempting to efface the memory of the splendid gold and silver brocade woven on the looms at Lyons. This fabric also covered the alcove walls, the two armchairs placed on either side of the bed, the twelve folding-stools and the curtains on the two windows. Under the mirror opposite the fireplace stood, in turn, three sumptuous commodes, none of which has been returned to Versailles.

It was in this room that Louis XV, stricken by smallpox, died on 10th May 1774. Louis XVI used his grandfather's bedchamber and, in 1788, ordered the Rousseau brothers to renovate the decoration of the dressing-room which is entered by a door behind the hangings in the alcove.

Chimneypiece in
Louis XV's bedchamber;
bust by A. Coysevox

After many changes, the Cabinet de la Pendule was given its present appearance in 1760. For the wall opposite the windows, Gabriel designed a magnificent set of four panels carved, like those of the bedchamber, by Jacques Verberckt, their rococo decoration echoed by the lively gilt arabesques above the cornice. When supper was held in the adjoining dining-room, the King and his guests would come here to finish the evening around a large number of games tables brought in for the occasion. Following Louis XIV's wishes, the Court continued to gamble for high stakes in the eighteenth century; fortunes were made in a matter of hours, but, on the other hand, players could be ruined and then had no choice but to hope for the King's generosity.

The magnificent set of furnishings has been returned here. Against the east wall stands Louis XV's great astronomical clock with its mechanism designed by the engineer Passemant and carried out by the clockmaker Dauthiau, protected by the splendid gilt bronze case by Caffiéri. Meticulously restored by Pierre Bécard, it still shows not only the hours but also the day and the month, the phase of the moon and the positions of the planets in the solar system.

Recently, the extraordinary gilt wood barometer, carved by Lemaire in 1773 for the future Louis XVI, was placed opposite the clock. Against the walls stand the four so-called "hunt" tables, commissioned by Louis XV between 1730 and 1757, their stucco tops showing the plans of the royal hunting estates.

Gabriel's Cabinet de la Pendule, with panelling by Jacques Verberckt

The clock by
C.S. Passemant and Dauthiau
in a case by J. Caffiéri

117

Beyond the Cabinet de la Pendule lies the marvellous room that used to be one of the most important rooms in the palace, not only because of the rôle it played, but also because of the quality of its decoration and furniture — Louis XV's study, called the Cabinet Intérieur.

From 1738 to 1760, Gabriel transformed Louis XIV's former Cabinet of Paintings by adorning it with sumptuous gilded panelling carved by Verberckt. Situated in a corner of the building, this jewel has the advantage of having both an easterly and southerly outlook; light flows in abundantly to add vibrancy to the gold of the wood-panelling and bronzes.

For his private study, Louis XV ordered the most splendid furniture ever made for the Crown. Each article is a masterpiece, the quality of which saved it from being sold during the sales of the Revolution. Preserved within France but scattered in various places, the furniture here has been brought together during the last twenty years after a great deal of effort, and bears witness, once again, to the supremacy of French art during the eighteenth century.

The oldest piece is the medal-chest delivered in 1739 by Gaudreaux and carried out from a design by the Slodtz brothers. It has two doors which hide the fourteen rosewood drawers inside which the King kept the medals struck by the Paris Mint in commemoration of the events of his reign. The marquetry is

Sèvres vases
and the medal-chest
by Antoine-Robert Gaudreaux

Louis XV's
Cabinet
Intérieur

embellished with gilt bronze ornamentation in which medals form garlands of flowers.

The two corner-cupboards are also medal-chests made by Joubert in 1755. Under Louis XVI, these three pieces of furniture, considered unfashionable, were given by the King to the royal library in Paris.

As for the roll-top writing-desk, it is rightly considered the greatest masterpiece of French cabinet-making. M. de Fontanieu, Superintendent of the "Royal Furniture Repository", had entrusted its execution to Oeben. The latter built the model, designed the ingenious mechanism that locks the roll-top and drawers, and finished the framework. When he died in 1765, Riesener was ordered to finish the work by clothing it in admirable marquetry and gilt bronze by Hervieux and Duplessis. The desk was delivered to the King in 1769 and did not leave this room until the Revolution.

Of the furniture from Louis XVI's time, six of the chairs carved by Foliot in 1774 and the clock bought from Roque in 1770 have been returned. Some time ago, to commemorate the bicentenary of American Independence, the exceptional ornaments by Thomire, commissioned by Louis XVI in 1785, were returned to Versailles — the two Sèvres vases and the candelabrum, jewels of porcelain and bronze.

Louis XV's roll-top desk
by Jean-François Oeben
and Jean-Henri Riesener

Here one often saw the most important persons at Court come to sign the marriage contracts of members of the royal family. When the affair of the "Queen's necklace" came to light, unjustly lowering the Queen's reputation in the eyes of the public, Louis XVI, in the presence of Marie-Antoinette and his ministers, summoned Cardinal de Rohan, who, during his interrogation, discovered that he had been tricked : the fabulous diamonds he thought he had bought for the Queen were in other hands...

"Your Eminence", said the King, "control yourself. To enable you to do so, and in order that the presence of the Queen and myself should not disturb your peace of mind, I suggest you proceed to the adjoining room. You will be alone there". The cardinal obeyed... returned, and handed a sheet of paper to the King. Taking it, His Majesty said, "I warn you that you shall be arrested". Bezenval thus relates the last act of this scandal in which the innocent Queen's reputation was ruined.

Pierre Philippe Thomire: the American Independence candelabrum

Cabinet Doré:
a panel by
Jacques Verbeckt

Until 1769, the King's Private Suite ended at the Annexe (a small study situated near the Cabinet Intérieur). Beyond it, until their regrettable destruction in 1752, lay the Ambassadors' Staircase and the sumptuous Small Gallery decorated by Mignard for Louis XIV. On their site, Gabriel was ordered to create an apartment for Madame Adélaïde, Louis XV's favorite daughter. This princess thus lived at her father's side for seventeen years.

1769 was an important date in Louis XV's private life. After having been a widower for a year, he had just met Madame du Barry, and installed her at the palace. The royal family made no effort to hide its disapproval of this liaison. The King arranged the move for his daughter to spare her any embarrassment, and he ordered the Private Suite to be enlarged by what were called the ''New Rooms'' from then on.

The first room is Madame Adélaïde's former Cabinet Doré. Its particularly rich decoration dates from 1767. It contains an admirable alcove with a mirror in the central pier, on either side of which Gabriel placed, in pairs, four of Verberckt's most extraordinary wood-panels, adorned with musical instruments, fishing tackle and gardening tools mingled with garlands of flowers and ribbons tied in bows. In this sumptuous setting, Madame Adélaïde took her music lessons from a teacher who was to become famous, Caron de Beaumarchais. One afternoon in December 1764, the royal family gathered here for a recital by a child virtuoso — Wolfgang Amadeus Mozart.

In 1769, Louis XV converted this drawing-room into a "coffee parlour" and had low glass cabinets placed along the walls to display the finest pieces of his gold plate.

Beyond it lay Madame Adélaïde's bedchamber, which Louis XV decided to turn into a games room. This room was completely transformed by Gabriel into a magnificent library on Louis XVI's accession to the throne.

Like all the members of the royal family, Louis XVI had received an extremely thorough education which developed his curiosity for the sciences and technology and encouraged his taste for learning. The most spectacular sign of Louis XVI's studious nature is undoubtedly the creation of this library which he wanted instantly and which is the only room at Versailles, apart from the little dressing-room belonging to the bedchamber, that he had transformed for his personal use.

The immense talent of the older Gabriel can be judged here. Nearly twenty years separate the creation of this décor from that of the preceding room. The architect's genius has not aged. The rococo style has given way to a neoclassical one, inspired by antiquity. Of Louis XVI's furniture, the table by Riesener and the terrestial globe were eventually returned here. The chest-of-drawers was replaced by one delivered to Versailles by Benneman for Monsieur, the King's brother.

Thanks to generous donations, the "painted Pekin silk" was recently rewoven and restores to the library the life, color and intimate charm of the past.

A musical trophy
by Jacques Verbeckt
from Mme Adélaïde's Cabinet Doré

Louis XVI's Library
with his globe and
the Riesener table

One set of library shelves is, in fact, a trompe-l'œil, and is the door through which one entered Madame Adélaïde's Grand Cabinet, later to become a dining-room under Louis XV and Louis XVI, and better known as the "Porcelain Room". This room is at present undergoing restoration.

The last room in this suite is Louis XVI's Games Room, which occupies the site of what was one of the wonders of Versailles under Louis XIV, his Cabinet des Médailles. Almost two-thirds of the furniture commissioned by Louis XVI and scattered during the Revolution has been returned to this room with its Louis XV decoration. The four superb corner-cupboards delivered by Riesener in 1774 have been returned to their original places and nineteen of the thirty-six chairs bought from Boulard in 1785 have been found again. A very rich silk fabric embroidered with gold covers the windows and chairs. All that is missing are the games tables which stood on the magnificent Savonnerie carpet with Louis XIV's initials.

Louis XVI's
Games
Room

125

The Private Apartments

Above the Private Suite, overlooking the Courtyard of the Stags and the entrance courtyards to the palace, lies the King's most secret domain at Versailles, the Private Apartments. Decorated by Gabriel for Louis XV, they consist of a series of small rooms with a fresh, charming décor, in which white or gilded wainscoting alternates with panels painted with *vernis Martin*, the famous lacquer perfected by the Martin brothers.

In this retreat, inaccessible to the courtiers, Louis XV would come to live simply, inviting a few friends to share his supper in one of the many dining-rooms. He also housed his mistresses here, including the two most celebrated ones, Madame de Pompadour and Madame du Barry. The Marquise lived for five years in the attic storey of the north wing before moving into a comfortable apartment on the ground-floor. In 1769, Comtesse du Barry moved into the section overlooking the Marble Courtyard and the Courtyard of the Stags. She lived there until Louis XV's death in 1774, receiving, in the company of the King, their faithful friends who had been invited to supper and games, attempting to forget all the rebuffs inflicted on her by the royal family and, in particular, by the young Dauphine, Marie-Antoinette. Her apartments consisted of a library, an antechamber, a games room, a drawing room, a dining-room and a bathroom. Very fine furniture has been placed in this suite, including the chairs by Foliot, called the "Furniture of the Gods".

Mme
du Barry's
library

The apartment
of
Mme du Barry

The Opera House

For more than a century, music and the theatre were at the center of the amusements which the King offered his courtiers at Versailles. The eighteenth century's passion for dramatic art is well-known. Great men and women of the time went on the boards themselves to perform for their friends. The one who did the most to encourage this fashion was Madame de Pompadour, who created her own troupe of actors and produced operas for the diversion of her royal lover. Later, Marie-Antoinette was to imitate the Marquise by creating the small theatre at Trianon.

When festivities were held, theatres sprang up all over the palace, gardens and outbuildings. Fate was against them, for the only ones remaining are Marie-Antoinette's theatre and, fortunately, the most beautiful of all, Louis XV's Opera House.

The Opera House, with painted set of the enlarged stage

It was for the marriage of his grandchildren, and, in particular, for that of the heir to the throne, that Louis XV commissioned Gabriel to build, in the palace, the large opera house that had been awaited since Louis XIV. The architect had very little time before him, only twenty-one months, but he had worked on the plans for many years and was able to meet the deadline set for the evening of 16th May 1770. The inauguration was a dazzling occasion. Louis XV held the royal banquet there following the celebration of the Dauphin's marriage to Marie-Antoinette.

The courtiers were as surprised as today's visitors by the luxury and elegance of Pajou's décor of carved wood, gilded or painted in imitation of marble. They also appreciated the modern elliptical ground-plan, imported from Italy, and the innovation of the levels graded in tiers. Gabriel had planned an opera house which could also be transformed into a large room for the holding of balls or banquets. On the 16th of May, the banqueting table was placed on a platform covering the orchestra pit, on a level with the stage. For balls, this area was doubled by creating another half-room at the back of the stage in a setting of colonnades. The dancers thus had a huge floor to whirl around on.

As the cost of producing theatrical works was very high, the Opera House was used only on a few very special occasions.

It was stripped during the Revolution and reopened under Louis-Philippe, and from 1870 to 1875 the Assembly and the Senate held their sessions there. From 1953 to 1957, large-scale renovations finally restored to the Opera House all its original glory.

The royal box

The curtain with the arms of France

131

The Hall of Battles, which fills the South Wing, is the most important creation in the Museum of French History, the work of Louis-Philippe.

One should not forget, however, when walking through it, that its construction entailed the complete destruction of some splendid apartments lived in by Monsieur, Louis XIV's brother, the Grand Dauphin and the Children of France.

In a setting designed by Nepveu and Fontaine, thirty huge paintings, eighty-two busts of soldiers and sixteen bronze plaques engraved with the names of heroes who had died for France form a magnificent summary of the history of our country.

From the battle of Tolbiac, won by Clovis, to Napoleon I's victory at Wagram in 1809, these paintings, commissioned by the "King of the French" from the most important artists of his time, offer us, through their evocative power and epic inspiration, an interesting epitome of the trends in nineteenth-century painting in France.

In the foreground:
"The battle of Taillebourg"
by Eugène Delacroix

THE MUSEUM

"To all the Glories of France":
the Hall of Battles
(390 feet long and 42 feet wide)

The Apartments of Madame de Maintenon

"The Water Theatre Grove"
by Jean Cotelle:
gouache in the bedchamber

Some months after the Queen's death, Louis XIV married Madame de Maintenon in the greatest secrecy. The Marquise had lived here, right opposite the King's apartments, since 1682, when the Court moved to Versailles; she remained until the Sun King's death in 1715.

This suite consists of four main rooms. The two antechambers hung with red damask contain the sixteenth century portraits from the Roger de Gaignières collection. In the bedchamber, which was changed beyond recognition in the nineteenth century, hang paintings dealing with the reign of good King Henri and an admirable series of gouaches by Jean Cotelle. In the drawing-room, adorned with furniture and objets d'art of exceptional quality, thanks to Doctor Roudinesco, the walls are covered with portraits of the prettiest ladies at Court.

The 17th Century Rooms

The Museum of French History, dedicated "To all the Glories of France", was inaugurated in 1837. Its creation entailed large-scale transformations of the palace interior, but had the advantage of enabling important collections from the sixteenth to the nineteenth centuries, torn from their original setting during the Revolution, to be brought together here. Since the turn of the century, on the initiative of Pierre de Nolhac, a constant effort has been made to improve this display of works of art and eliminate copies.

The North Wing was chosen for the exhibition of seventeenth century works, hung on cloth backgrounds decorated with antique motifs. They are presented in chronological order to illustrate the reigns of Louis XIII and Louis XIV. Each room displays a different theme and the whole collection offers us a remarkable testimony to a dazzling civilization.

Louis XIV
the young sovereign,
painted by Charles Le Brun

Among the subjects illustrated one should mention the Jansenist movement of Port-Royal, Louis XIV's foreign policy, the Court and the development of the arts and sciences. One of the rooms is almost entirely dedicated to the painter Pierre Mignard. A great rival of Le Brun, on the latter's death he was named First Painter to the King, thanks to the powerful protection of Louvois, the Superintendent of Buildings. His chief work at Versailles was the creation of the Small Gallery behind the Ambassadors' Staircase. This, too, was unfortunately destroyed on the orders of Louis XV in 1752.

Among the best known of its paintings the museum includes that of the "Grand Dauphin and his family", commissioned in 1687 for the Queen's bedchamber. Louis XIV's son, who was the "son of a king, father of kings, but never himself a king", as Saint-Simon's well-known saying goes, is leaning on the table, nonchalantly patting a dog. At his side his wife, the Dauphine Marie-Anne of Bavaria, holds on a stool her new-born child, the Duc de Berry. Seated on a cushion at his mother's feet, a charming little child with blonde curls seems to be lost in daydreams. He is the Duc d'Anjou, whom destiny was to call to the throne of Spain in 1700. Standing with a spear in his hand is the Duc de Bourgogne, the eldest grandson of France who was to be the father of Louis XV.

These remarkable figures of children make this painting one of the masterpieces of seventeenth century French portraiture.

Taken during the Revolution, this painting was bought back by Louis XVIII and returned to Versailles in 1960. It has been given a place of honour in the museum, as it could not be displayed in the Salon de Mars, where it used to hang in the seventeenth century.

"The Grand Dauphin
and his family"
by Pierre Mignard

137

The first floor of the North Wing also contains various rooms dedicated to war, the arts and the royal family. One of these has been set aside for the four panoramic paintings by Adam Van der Meulen depicting episodes from the War of Devolution and commissioned for the King's Pavilion at the château of Marly. In his accurate rendering of war-scenes, Van der Meulen has succeeded in blending the atmosphere and poetry of the great expanses of cloudy sky of northern France. The entry of Louis XIV and Marie-Thérèse into Arras, where we see the Queen in her superb carriage, glittering with gold, is the work of the same artist.

With the Sun King, the Court reached a degree of splendour hitherto unknown. Louis XIV, who dressed with great simplicity, wished his courtiers always to be clothed as richly as possible. The setting for this luxury was that of the royal residences which the sovereign had renovated or newly built. To fulfil this aim, he encouraged the artists of the Académie Française, whose paintings for their admission to this royal institution hang in several rooms of the museum. Those by Martin and Allegrain have preserved for us the picture of Louis XIV's favorite residences after Versailles — Vincennes, Saint-Germain-en-Laye, Trianon and Marly. To these must be added the interesting view of the château of Saint-Cloud, the residence of Monsieur, the King's brother, which was burnt down in 1870.

As we know, the end of the reign was saddened by unfortunate wars and a large number of deaths in the royal family. However, the smile of a young woman poured a little happiness into the old King's heart. She was his granddaughter, Marie-Adélaïde of Savoy, the Duchesse de Bourgogne and later Dauphine of France. Gobert has left us with a portrait of Louis XV's mother, dressed for a hunt, all in red, smiling and gracious. This unfortunate princess was to die in 1712, followed several days later by her husband and eldest son — a succession of deaths that plunged the whole country into deep sorrow.

The Duchesse de Bourgogne: painting by Pierre Gobert

A wood nymph in terracotta, by Antoine Coysevox, and a view of the first floor rooms

Adam Van der Meulen:
"Entry of Queen Marie-Thérèse
in Arras" (detail)

140

Louis XIV is shown
riding the white horse
immediately behind the coach

The most striking sign of the magnificence of Louis XIV's reign remains the creation of the château of Versailles, abundantly illustrated by a whole series of views by Van der Meulen, Patel and Martin, who seem to have followed each stage of construction step by step.

André Le Nôtre brought to the art of garden design an altogether new splendour. A colossal pumping mechanism with an aqueduct was built at Marly to supply water for the fountains.

Under the reign of Louis XIV, France reached the heights of military, economic and cultural power. The last room is dedicated to "the glory of the Sun King". A large tapestry cartoon by Hallé (shown on page 240) illustrates French predominance at the end of the seventeenth century. The scene is that of the reparation made to Louis XIV in 1685 by the Doge of Genoa in the Hall of Mirrors. The King, standing before his silver throne, is surrounded by the Grand Dauphin, the Duc d'Orléans and the princes of the royal family.

Versailles:
the château around 1668,
painted by Pierre Patel

Near the reservoirs,
the grotto
of Tethys

The 18th Century Rooms

Since 1900, when Pierre de Nolhac began to reorganize the museum, the whole eighteenth century collection has been gathered on the ground floor of the château's main building in the rooms disfigured by Louis-Philippe and which, during the Ancien Régime, were among the principal apartments in the palace.

These consisted, in succession, of the former apartments of the Dauphine and Dauphin, those of Mesdames, the daughters of Louis XV, Madame de Pompadour's second set of apartments and Marie-Antoinette's private apartment.

In addition to a number of precious paintings by Nattier, Rigaud, Van Loo, Drouais, Vigée-Lebrun and Labille-Guiard, these rooms also contain a unique collection of furniture signed by the greatest cabinet-makers of the time. Many pieces originally came from the royal residences or were once the property of princes.

The Dauphin's library,
with panelling and commode
painted in ''vernis Martin''

The
Dauphin's
bedchamber

The Dauphine's apartments were considerably altered during Louis XVI's time to lodge the Dauphin, and what remained of them was destroyed by Louis-Philippe. Only the annexe could be restored. The carved cornice and the remaining wainscoting, completed by new panels, have been repainted in the fresh colors of the famous *vernis Martin*. A fine organ in a carved case which probably belonged to Madame Adélaïde has been returned to the disfigured antechamber. On the walls of these rooms hang paintings depicting the Regency and the beginnings of Louis XV's reign, including a delightful portrait of Louis XV as a child, painted by Rigaud.

In the Dauphin's apartments, the decoration of the library and bedchamber has been restored. In the 1747 room, the panelling designed by Gabriel and executed by Verberckt has been returned, thus giving full value to the mantelpiece with its astonishing figures of sculpted bronze. The overdoors painted by Pierre and dedicated to the history of Venus have also been put back here. A new suite of furniture bearing the signatures of Chennevat, Delanois, Foliot and Heurtaut has restored this room to its former importance. In the alcove two masterpieces by Nattier are displayed — portraits of Mesdames Henriette and Adélaïde as goddesses.

Nattier was the favorite painter of the great ladies of the time. No one could bring out the grace of his models better than he. He launched the fashion of mythological portraits, draped in satins of cool colors which illuminate the beauty of a face. Versailles possesses the biggest collection of this master's works, to which the lower gallery is dedicated.

Marie-Josèphe of Saxony,
the mother of three Kings of France:
painting by Jean-Marc Nattier

The family of
the Marquis de Sourches:
painting by François-Hubert Drouais

146

Beyond the lower gallery extends a series of rooms, at right angles to the northern section of the main building. Their destiny was a particularly glorious one. It was here that Le Vau and Le Brun created what was without a doubt one of the most amazing wonders of Versailles — Louis XIV's Appartement des Bains. The rooms were panelled with rare marbles, adorned with magnificent sculptures and gilt bronzes and embellished with paintings by Houasse and Lemoine.

This room disappeared little by little during the eighteenth century, altered when occupied by Madame Victoire, the Marquise de Pompadour and, after the latter's death, by Madame Adélaïde until 1789.

The paintings and furniture date from the end of Louis XV's reign and the beginning of Louis XVI's accession. In the vestibule, with its Dinan marble columns, hangs a work by François-Hubert Drouais. The Marquis de Sourches, the Great Provost of France, with his wife and children are preparing to make music. The scene takes place in an enchanting natural setting and enables the artist to create a masterpiece of freshness and poetry evoking that pleasant art of living which characterized the eighteenth century.

The following rooms contain some fine portraits and an exceptional suite of furniture created by Jacob in 1785 for Marie-Antoinette. The former antechambers of Madame de Pompadour and Madame Adélaïde, destroyed by Louis-

The Salle des Hocquetons
(Room of the Archers)
with bronze copy of the Apollo Belvedere

Philippe, were restored from 1953 to 1955 to their Louis XIV state. This revealed a precious remnant from the Ambassadors' Staircase — the Salle des Hocquetons, (Room of the Archers) with its trompe-l'œil décor in gold and *grisaille* adorned with real or artificial niches. The original gilded doors by Delobel, submerged in the eighteenth century stonework, were found again.

This room is used today to display one of the most extraordinary clocks in Versailles, the one called "the creation of the world" clock, whose mechanism was designed by Passemant and carried out by Roque. Its sumptuous gilt and silverplated bronze ornamentation is a masterpiece by François-Thomas Germain.

Dupleix commissioned this clock for the King of Golconda, but when in 1754 the governor-general of the Compagnie des Indes was recalled, he kept the clock. His heirs sold it to the State in 1796.

The astronomical mechanism was entirely restored by the Lepaute brothers in 1807.

The "creation of the world" clock

"Bonaparte crossing the Alps at
the Great Saint Bernard Pass":
copy by Langlois after J.-L. David

150

Consulate and Empire

Having chosen to live in the former royal residences which had been left empty by the Revolution, Napoleon I felt obliged to have them refurnished and redecorated. Large numbers of paintings were thus commissioned. This documentary collection, placed in reserve by Louis XVIII, was saved from oblivion by Louis-Philippe who decided to use it for the Museum of French History.

Before mounting the "stucco staircase" to the rooms of the southern attic, the visitor has to pass through one of the most popular creations in the Museum — the Coronation Room. It owes its name to the two large historical paintings placed here by Louis-Philippe — the "Coronation of the Empress" and the "Distribution of Eagle Standards", commissioned by the Emperor from Jacques-Louis David. The former of these paintings was sent to the Louvre in 1889. It has been replaced by a copy painted by the artist himself during his exile in Brussels.

"Coronation
of the Empress"
by Jacques-Louis David

151

"Entry of the French
into Berlin,
27 October 1806"

Painting
by
Charles Meynier

153

The reorganization of this collection made possible the inauguration, in 1970, of the "southern attics" which complement the "Louis-Philippe Rooms", situated on the ground-floor of the South Wing and reserved for large paintings. These rooms contain paintings of small or medium size as well as gouaches, drawings and watercolors. Others were purchased to fill certain gaps and, to evoke the Empire atmosphere, the paintings are hung on fabrics woven from examples designed for the imperial palaces, from which the furniture and objets d'art also come.

Antoine-Jean Gros became famous for his painting "Napoleon visiting the plague-stricken at Jaffa", displayed in the 1804 salon and now hung in the Louvre. We also owe him the legendary work "Bonaparte on the bridge at Arcole", depicting the remarkable act of daring during the first Italian campaign.

Several fine pencil studies by David, and his portrait of Pius VII, precede a chef-d'œuvre by the master — "Bonaparte crossing the Alps at the Great Saint Bernard Pass". As the hero had wished, David portrayed him sitting "calmly on a

The wedding procession
entering the Tuileries:
painting by E. B. Garnier

154

spirited steed"; this memorable feat, which took place on 20th May 1800, was one of the major events of the second Italian campaign.

Baron François Gérard was the most sought-after portrait-painter of the time — "the king of painters and the painter of kings". Versailles is the proud possessor of a dazzling set of miniature portraits of famous persons, known as Gérard's "sketches". In fact, they are copies painted from full-size originals which he had been commissioned to do. Intellectual life is conjured up by the most celebrated personalities of the time.

Standing before the portraits of the imperial family, it is easy to imagine the luxury of this new Court. Farther on, the third Coalition, illustrated by the victory of Austerlitz on 2nd December 1805, and the Prussian and Polish campaigns, of which the "Entry of the French into Berlin" (by Meynier) is an episode, mark the various stages in this Great Epic. Then there is a series of excellent compositions showing us Marie-Louise, the future Empress — her "Departure from Vienna" (by Auzou), her "Arrival at Compiègne", the "Entry of the procession into the Tuileries" (by Garnier), the marriage ceremony in the Square Drawing-Room of the Louvre (by Rouget), and, finally, the sumptuous banquet held on the evening of 2nd April 1810.

Other attentive witnesses were Bagetti and Baron Lejeune. Versailles has a unique set of gouaches depicting events which took place outside France painted by Bagetti, an engineer-topographer from Piedmont in the service of France. We owe to Napoleon III the presence here of the works by Lejeune. An artist who became a general, he took part in all the campaigns of the Empire.

In 1813, almost all of Europe joined forces to defeat France. On 20th October 1814, before leaving for exile on the island of Elba, the heir of the Revolution bade farewell to the Imperial Guard. The last paintings portray the death-throes of this glorious epic — the Hundred Days, which ended on 18th June 1815 at Waterloo, and the end of the Eagle imprisoned on the islet of Saint Helena.

"Farewell to the Imperial Guard" by A. A. Montfort

The Fountain of Apollo
seen against the
Grand Canal

THE GARDENS

The sculptures in lead
by J. S. Tuby
were originally gilded

The west façade
and Fountain
of Diana

159

The gardens of Versailles are the perfect model of the "French Garden" whose origins are attributed to André Le Nôtre. This somewhat simplified view requires further comment.

The symmetrical organization of the garden around a main axis, the symbolism of the statues and the water gushing forth abundantly certainly already existed in Renaissance Italy, the finest example being the Belvedere gardens in the Vatican, designed by Bramante. Their influence spread to France, along the Loire valley and, in particular, to Amboise, famous for its geometrical parterres, but which is a flat garden with no terraces.

At Versailles, under Louis XIII, Jacques de Menours had laid out the great east-west axis before Le Nôtre and, according to the fashion of the time, had created a multiplicity of *"compartiments de broderie"*, patterns of flowers shaped by clipped box hedging and by ground colored with fine gravel and crushed brick or slate.

Vase de la Guerre:
magnificent sculpture
by Antoine Coysevox

160

The river Loire:
bronze from the Parterre d'Eau
by Thomas Regnaudin

Le Nôtre's stroke of genius both at Versailles and Vaux-le-Vicomte, was to enlarge the gardens and break their monotony by using the slopes and unevenness of the ground to their fullest advantage. Thus the hill of Versailles was modelled into terraces, steps or great staircases. He also carefully created a transition between the stone of the building and the beds of flowers by means of expanses of water in which the foliage is reflected. The waters of the brooks, springs and marshes were drained into the fountains, but soon this was no longer sufficient despite a gigantic pump at Clagny, and Arnold de Ville's project had to be adopted. Thus the fantastic *Machine de Marly* was created.

Bramante had the most famous classical statues placed in the Belvedere gardens, but these bore no iconographical relationship to each other. At Versailles, on the other hand, one looks at the statues as one would read the pages of a book on mythology. Charles Le Brun with Le Nôtre designed a symbolic representation of the solar myth, and thus dedicated the east-west axis to Apollo. The statues, designed after drawings by Le Brun, illustrate Ovid's *Metamorphoses*. Among them were placed fine copies of classical statues.

Despite the disappearance of several very fine groves, the gardens and park of Versailles continue to reveal Le Nôtre's genius, so well described by La Fontaine: "He had the power to command Nature; she obeyed him because he asked of her what she was able to give."

"Air" by
Etienne Le Hongre
from the Fountain of Diana

"Noon" by
G. Marsy from
the Fountain of Diana

The Parterre d'Eau

The Parterre d'Eau was given its name when Mansart created the two large pools which Le Nôtre had designed. The water provides both a continuation of the beautiful façade reflected in it and the beginning of a panorama which ends in another, even greater expanse of water, the Grand Canal.

At the corners of the terrace of the château's main building, beneath the windows of the Salon de la Guerre and the Salon de la Paix, two massive marble vases illustrate these same themes. At the foot of the façade four statues cast in bronze after classical works form a link between the statues of the buildings and that of the two pools.

On the rims round the edges of the pools lie outstretched bronze statues representing the rivers of France, nymphs, and, at the corners, four groups of children playing. The work of several famous sculptors, the statues are in perfect harmony with the great façades of the château.

To the west, the Parterre d'Eau is flanked by the raised pools of the Fountain of the Animals, also called the fountains of Diana and Daybreak after two of their statues. The bronzes of fighting animals, cast, like those of the Parterre d'Eau, by the Keller brothers, are a precious testimony to seventeenth century animal sculpture.

Central section
of the château
and the Parterre d'Eau

Children playing:
group from the south pool
by Pierre Granier

The Parterre of Latona

A flight of steps between gentle slopes leads from the Parterre d'Eau to the Parterre of Latona. The two slopes are adorned with vases, the most famous being those at the top of this majestic staircase. These are the Vases of the Sun, with the emblem of Louis XIV as a central motif — the smiling face of a young god with a halo of rays.

Below lies the pool of Latona, in its center four concentric marble basins rising up to the group carved by Balthazar Marsy, "Latona and her children". We see illustrated here the legend according to which the goddess, the mother of Apollo and Diana, implores Jupiter on her knees to take revenge upon the Lycian peasants who had treated her disrespectfully. At an order from Jupiter, they are turned into frogs.

In the center of the two parterres which lie on either side of the central avenue, the Fountains of Lizards continue the metamorphosis theme and are adorned with half-human, half-batrachian figures in lead by the Marsy brothers. These parterres are edged with fine marble vases, certain of which are copies of classical ones and, at either extremity, with two statues — to the north "The Nymph with a shell", from the original by Coysevox, and, to the south, "The dying gladiator", a copy of a famous classical statue.

The Fountain of Latona
and view along the Tapis Vert
to the Grand Canal

The Pool of Latona,
with all the
fountains playing

167

The two slopes flanking the Parterre of Latona are each broken by nine marble statues, certain of which were carved from drawings by Le Brun. The others are copies of famous classical statues carved in the seventeenth century by the students of the Academy of France in Rome.

These slopes lead finally to a semi-circle adorned with a number of terms representing gods or philosophers and marble groups such as "Castor and Pollux", by Coysevox or "Laocoön and his sons", by Tuby. Two masterpieces by Puget, the "Milon of Croton" and "Perseus saving Andromeda", which once stood at the beginning of the Tapis Vert, are today in the Louvre. This spot is called the Point de Vue, for it was here that Louis XIV asked his visitors to pause for a moment so that they could admire the different views of his gardens: the façade of the château to the east, the Grand Canal to the west, and, to the north and south, the pools of Ceres and Bacchus reached by shaded paths.

A marble vase from
the Parterre of Latona
by Jean Cornu

"Laocoön and his sons":
copy from the antique
by Jean-Baptiste Tuby

The Royal Avenue, which is the central and most important section of the east-west axis, rolls out its carpet of wide lawn — hence its other name — from the Parterre of Latona to the Fountain of Apollo.

The two paths beside the Tapis Vert are lined with statues and large carved urns, and bordered by tall trees.

The figures, consisting of original works and copies of classical sculptures, were carved in the seventeenth century. They include the "Medici Venus", "Artemis", "Dido", "Achilles at Scyros" and "Cyparisse", an expressive work by Flamen showing Apollo's young favorite bending over the deer he loved so tenderly.

Twelve monumental urns accent this majestic ensemble. The noble elegance of their decoration, with the royal initials, cornucopias or sun flowers, attests to the mastery of the sculptors of Versailles.

The Royal Avenue

"Cyparisse caressing his fawn" by Anselme Flamen

A marble vase with sunflowers

In the center of the half-moon adorned with terms and statues, the Fountain of Apollo occupies the site of Louis XIII's former round pool or Rondeau. Louis XIV first had it transformed into the Fountain of the Swans and then, in 1671, as part of the symbolism of the gardens, it became an essential point in the east-west axis. The magnificent composition by Tuby, once covered in gold, could be seen glistening from the palace.

Executed from a drawing by Le Brun, who was inspired by a painting by Albani, this remarkable composition illustrates the beginning of the Sun God's journey as he rises from the waters on a chariot drawn by four spirited steeds. Around him, tritons and dolphins announce the return of day.

The water from this fountain creates, as it gushes forth, majestic fleurs-de-lis which rise towards the sky.

The Fountain of Apollo

The Sun God
riding
his horses

"...they create the dew
by tossing their manes"
(La Fontaine)

The Grand Canal, which continues the east-west axis, extends the main view of the gardens towards infinity. In the center it is intersected by an arm, thus forming the shape of a cross. One could embark here for the Menagerie which lay to the south or for the Grand Trianon to the north.

During the sumptuous Court festivities the canal was the scene of fireworks and lighting displays. One of the most celebrated of these was held in 1674.

There was also a flotilla of gondolas, a gift from the Republic of Venice, and the gondoliers were housed near the canal in a group of low houses which were called "Little Venice" from that time on.

The King's private fleet which sailed on this immense canal consisted of two large gilded galliots, nine shallops and the "Great Galley" which was hung with crimson brocade edged with fleurs-de-lis.

During the severe winters, groups of skaters and sleigh races continued to fill the Grand Canal with life.

"Apollo"
in the main axis
continued by the Grand Canal

174

The Grand Canal

The Grand Trianon
arm of the canal,
near the Menagerie

The Parterre du Nord

As we leave the main axis dedicated to the legend of Apollo and come back to the great façade, we should look to the left of the Parterre d'Eau. A broad flight of steps leading to the Parterre du Nord is flanked by two copies of classical statues cast in bronze. These are the "Knife-grinder", by Foggini, and the "Modest Venus", by Coysevox. The coping on either side holds fine bronze vases, most of which are by Claude Ballin, Louis XIV's goldsmith.

The parterre, consisting of stretches of lawn edged with flower-beds, is protected from cold winds by huge trees as well as by the North Wing with its massive architecture. The parterre is decorated with several marble vases and two circular pools called the Crown Fountains. The work of Le Hongre and Tuby, these are composed of sirens and tritons. Laughing nonchalantly, the little marine gods swim under the shower of the falling water. They once held a large crown of laurel leaves in each pool. Cast in lead, all these figures formerly gleamed with a veneer of gilt.

The paths lining this parterre to the west and north display a magnificent set of statues and terms, the majority of which were created as part of the great 1674 commission of sculptures for the Parterre d'Eau. They illustrate the following themes: the four seasons, the four corners of the world, the four parts of the day, the four types of poetry, the four humours of man. Some, like "Winter", by Girardon, or "Night", by Raon, with its mysterious smile, are true masterpieces of sculpture.

Siren and tritons
from the Crown Fountain
by J. B. Tuby and E. Le Hongre

"Night"
by Jean Raon,
and the bird of darkness

The Pyramid Fountain and the Bathing Nymphs

The central avenue of the Parterre du Nord leads to the Pyramid Fountain by Girardon, made between 1669 and 1672 from a drawing by Le Brun. This once gilded masterpiece in lead is like a "little temple to the glory of water". From a vase adorned with the heads of satyrs at the top gushes a powerful jet of water which descends in a cascade into four superimposed shallow bowls held aloft by tritons, dolphins and crayfish.

The "Bathing Nymphs", just beyond the Pyramid, is a square pool with three of its walls adorned with bas-reliefs separated by terms. The fourth, and most important, wall was carved by Girardon and shows eleven nymphs joyfully splashing about in the waters of a river. It is framed by carvings of rivers and children; on the side walls, nymphs, cupids and dolphins accompany this charming scene.

The Pyramid Fountain
by François Girardon
from a design by C. Le Brun

"Bathing Nymphs": detail
from lead bas-relief
by François Girardon

The Allée des Marmosets

After the ''Bathing Nymphs'' by Girardon, the Water Walk or Allée des Marmousets offers us the child-like grace of joyful infants dancing in the shade of century-old trees.

It was probably designed by Claude Perrault around 1668, at the same time as the Pyramid Fountain and the ''Bathing Nymphs''. Fourteen groups of children were first placed opposite each other along this walk which leads to the Dragon Fountain. Later, eight others were added and took their places around the semi-circle opening onto the Fountain of Neptune. First executed in lead, the sculptures were later cast in bronze, in 1684, and it is in this form that they still enchant us today.

The theme of childhood can be seen everywhere, but each subject here is treated differently — there are tritons, cupids, child musicians, young fishermen or hunters, or carefree little dancers. The figures are all grouped in threes, each group in the center of a round, white marble pool, holding a bowl of pink marble from the middle of which a spray of water flows down onto the children. Originally, these bowls were filled with flowers and fruit of gilded lead, which have since disappeared.

The designs for these graceful figures were the work of Le Brun. However, the artists who created them — Le Gros, Le Hongre, Lerambert, Mazeline and Buirette — brought to them their personal talent which has left its imprint on the works of each of the sculptures in the gardens.

''Bathing Nymphs''
by François Girardon:
the central motif

Children dancing:
fountain from the
Allée des Marmousets

182

The Allée des Marmousets leads us to the Dragon Fountain which lies in the axis of the shady slope. A symbol of the victory of Apollo over Python, the monster with spread wings is surrounded by dolphins in the midst of which swim swans ridden by little cupids preparing for combat with bows and arrows.

The Fountain of Neptune, begun in the seventeenth century by Le Nôtre and continued by Mansart, lies in a semi-circle. The retaining wall is adorned with urns and shells. Below it in the water are three fine sculptural groups placed here during the time of Louis XV. The central group, by the artist L.S. Adam, represents Neptune and Amphitrite. On either side, J.B. Lemoine and E. Bouchardon created the Ocean seated upon on a sea monster, and Proteus leaning on a unicorn.

At each side of the pool is a cupid, perched astride a dragon.

Ninety-nine jets of water spray from all these statues to create an impressive and unforgettable sight.

''The Ocean'',
sea god
by J. B. Lemoine

The Fountain of Neptune

"Neptune and Amphitrite":
the central group
of the fountain

We must now go back along the Allée des Marmousets and to the other end of the main façade. Here, by a flight of steps leading to the Parterre du Midi, are two bronze cupids. The work of Sarrazin, these little spirits are among the oldest statues to be found at Versailles. Lerambert carved the marble sphinxes on which they are placed.

This parterre extends as far as the end of the Queen's Apartments. It is very simply decorated with two plain circular pools and arabesques of box-tree, abundantly adorned with flowers in summer, on either side of the central pathway.

Several marble vases and, in particular, small vases of sculptured bronze stand on the coping-stone round the parterre. In the summer, these urns are filled with geraniums in pink or the brightest red, vividly contrasting with the mellow stone of the château.

On the balustrade of the steps leading down to the Orangery lies "Ariadne sleeping", a marble copy by Van Clève of a classical statue in the Vatican.

Bronze vase
by Calla at the
edge of the parterre

The Parterre du Midi

Floral embroidery
and box-tree scrolls
with the Orangery beyond

The
Parterre
du Midi

189

At the end of the Parterre du Midi, a balustrade on either side leads us to two majestic staircases, each of one hundred steps, framing the Orangery by Mansart, situated below. This building replaced Le Vau's small orangery; of colossal size, it consists of a main gallery, 504 feet long, flanked by two others, each 372 feet

long. The entrances are marked by massive columns and the main façade is lit by thirteen huge arched windows.

Intended to shelter the exotic plants during the cold weather, this building contained up to 2000 orange trees and 1000 oleanders, pomegranates or palm-trees. During the warm season they decorate the avenues of the parterre delimited by the Hundred Steps and composed of a large circular pool surrounded by beds of flowers and stretches of lawn. To the south, a terrace overlooks the lake dug in 1679 by the regiment of Swiss Guards. Like the Grand Canal, which continues the east-west view of the gardens, the vast mirror of this sheet of water extends the north-south axis as far as the wooded horizon.

The Orangery Parterre
by J. H. Mansart,
and the Hundred Steps

The Royal Orangery

The south front
of the huge
Orangery

191

The artificial rocks and ruin
created in 1778
by Hubert Robert

192

The Groves

After admiring from the first floor of the palace the great panoramas stretching out before us — wide expanses glorifying Apollo or the deities of the waters — we must now penetrate the wooded thickets lined with paths parallel to the principal axes.

This immense foliage contains a series of well-hidden groves used for many purposes — as ballroom, refreshment room, theatre and art gallery, or simply as a setting for the joy of the wanderer. Such are the Baths of Apollo, an ingenious setting created for Girardon's group, "Apollo tended by Nymphs". Far removed in taste from the severity of the Grand Siècle, this grotto by Hubert Robert, an oasis in the "English Garden" of Louis XVI's time, offers the contrast of its cool greenery to the wanderer who has arrived here from the vast sunny parterres.

These small, open-air glades were for the most part used as if they were rooms. They were actually furnished and decorated, like the drawing-rooms in the palace itself, with "chests-of-drawers, pedestal-tables, vases and rich candlestands".

A large number of them have unfortunately gone, such as the Tree Fountains, or the sumptuous grove of the Triumphal Arch, but those we can still see today enable us to conjure up the splendour and magnificence of the festivities once held there.

The setting for
"Apollo tended
by Nymphs"

At the foot of the Latona Parterre, on either side of the entrance to the Tapis Vert, were once two groves with fountains — the Chandelier Grove and the Dolphin Grove. Louis XIV mentions them in the itinerary he suggests for visiting the gardens; he advises a "pause" to admire the "Bouquet of Groves". These were replaced by two quincunxes adorned with terms carved from drawings by Poussin.

To the left of Latona, hidden by the trees, the Rockwork Grove, once called the "Ballroom", displays its iridescent colors and its golds. The central section held a dance-floor surrounded by a ditch decorated with shells. This arena has gone but the steps on which the Court sat and the rockwork creating a cascade still remain. The water sparkled in the light of the crystal candelabra placed on candlestands at the foot of the steps. On the upper level the orchestra played among vases of gilt lead.

To the south of the Rockwork Grove used to lie the Labyrinth with its meandering paths sprayed by the water from thirty-nine fountains. Trellis alcoves held animals from Aesop's fables, realistically painted lead sculptures. Destroyed in 1775, it was replaced by the Queen's Grove, decorated with several statues and terms, including the "Fighting Gladiator", a statue of Minerva and a Capitoline Aphrodite.

The Capitoline
Aphrodite in
the Queen's Grove

Vase by E. Le Hongre and
L. Lecomte from
the Rockwork Grove

Autumn and Winter

Returning towards the southern quincunx, we arrive at the Fountain of Autumn; octagonal in shape, it holds in its center a group in which Bacchus sits smiling amidst the gathered grapes, surrounded by young satyrs playing with bunches of grapes. It was executed by the Marsy brothers after a drawing by Le Brun.

The Fountain of Winter, farther along the same pathway, was also designed by Le Brun and executed by Girardon. Here Saturn is shown as an old man who has had majestic wings from time immemorial, surrounded by cupids who bring their gaiety to the cold season as they play with bellows or shells.

Between Saturn and the Colonnade lies a grove called the "Hall of Chestnut Trees" on a site of the former "Hall of Antiques". To the south lies the Half-Moon Pool and the King's Garden, planted by Louis XVIII on the site of the Isle of Love.

"Saturn", or the Fountain of Winter, by François Girardon

"Bacchus", or the Fountain of Autumn, by the Marsy brothers

199

The Colonnade was built by Mansart in 1685 on the site of what was formerly the Parterre des Sources.

The circular peristyle consists of thirty-two columns of slate-blue or pink Languedoc marble, paired with the same number of pilasters, supporting the arcade and cornice in white marble. On the spandrels of the arches are carved bas-reliefs representing children playing; some weave crowns and garlands of flowers, whilst others play the lute, the lyre, the violin or the tambourin. These little musicians remind us that the groves were used for a great number of concerts as well as suppers and light meals during the festivities, many of which were held at night. In each archway stands a white marble bowl with a jet of water spouting from its center.

In 1699, Louis XIV had Girardon's famous group, ''The rape of Persephone by Pluto'', placed here, but this masterpiece had to be removed from the grove as a consequence of its having unfortunately begun to deteriorate.

The Colonnade
by
J. H. Mansart

Spring and Summer

Let us now cross the Tapis Vert and pass Apollo's chariot to take the path leading to the Fountain of Spring. On the right lies the Grove of the Domes. Once called the Fountain of Fame after the figure which decorated the central pool, it got its present name in 1677 when Mansart built two domed pavilions of white marble here, which were destroyed in the nineteenth century.

The Fountain of Spring is circular in shape, with a group carved in lead by Tuby in its center — Flora surrounded by cupids is seated, half-naked, amidst flowers.

As we go back towards the palace, we come to the Fountain of Summer which rounds off the perfect quadrilateral of the seasons. This octagonal pool represents Ceres, crowned with ears of corn, in the company of three young cupids who relax happily, lying on the sheaves of corn. This group is by Regnaudin.

"Flora", or the
Fountain of Spring,
by J. B. Tuby

202

"Ceres", or the
Fountain of Summer,
by Thomas Regnaudin

"Apollo tended
by Nymphs" by
F. Girardon and
T. Regnaudin

One of the most important groves at Versailles is that of the Baths of Apollo, which holds the groups created for the famous Grotto of Tethys destroyed when the North Wing was built. The central group, "Apollo tended by Nymphs", is the work of Girardon and Regnaudin — the Sun God, tired after his journey, is seated and the handmaidens of Tethys crowd around him. This admirable composition is accompanied by two groups by Marsy and Guérin, representing the Sun Horses being groomed by tritons.

On the site of this grove once stood the Pièce du Marais devised by Madame de Montespan "in which a metal tree could be seen spouting water from all its branches". In 1701 Mansart erected gilded canopies to cover three groups which, after the destruction of the grotto, had been temporarily displayed in the Grove of the Domes. In 1778, Hubert Robert, ordered to replant the park, designed a new plan for it. The fashion at the beginning of Louis XVI's reign was that of the landscape garden; he therefore had a small lake dug and lined its bank with a

The
Enceladus
Fountain

huge artificial rock containing grottoes and adorned with columns. This was the new palace of Tethys which still charms us today.

Let us take the avenue of Ceres and Flora once more, then cross diagonally towards the Fountain of Apollo. There, hidden in a thicket, is the great Fountain of Enceladus. This huge lead sculpture represents the giant crushed by the rocks of Mount Olympus which he had attempted to scale with his companions to reach heaven. This scene seems to have been inspired by the fresco by Giulio Romano in Mantua. The very fine head, four times larger than life, recalls that of the hero of the "Fall of the Titans". The powerful jet that spouts from his mouth rises to a height of seventy-five feet.

To the north-east of the Enceladus Fountain is the Obelisk Fountain, built by Mansart in 1706 on the site of the Council Room or Banqueting Hall. From the center of a clump of reeds rise two hundred and thirty jets of water forming a pyramid eighty-one feet high.

"Fall of Titan" by G. Marsy

Following a line due east towards the Parterre du Nord from the Obelisk, we pass first through the Star Grove, formerly called the Mountain of Water. Originally adorned with a pool containing numerous fountains, in 1704 it was turned into a simple grove of five paths in the shape of a star.

To the right of the Fountains of Spring and Summer, going towards the château, lies the northern quincunx. Like those in its southern counterpart, its terms come from Vaux-le-Vicomte: Flora, Summer, Pan and Bacchus to the south; Abundance, Liberality, Winter and a Faun to the north.

As we cross the path once more near the Fountain of Ceres we come to the Island of Children. In the center of the pool rises a rock on which little cupids frolic and pluck rose petals whilst others gambol in the water. Carved by Hardy for the Porcelain Trianon, they were placed here in 1710.

To the east of this pool, the Green Ring has replaced the Water Theatre created by Le Nôtre. The latter's hyd-

A young faun
from the northern
quincunx

raulic effects, "in the shape of cradles or sheaves", mingled with each other among groups of gilded lead. Destroyed in the eighteenth century, this grove has been replaced by a simple lawn bowl.

Two other features should be mentioned before leaving these gardens of Versailles: the wonderful groves, now sadly overgrown, that lay on either side of the Allée des Marmousets and were a magnificent reflection of the pomp of the Grand Siècle. These were the Grove of the Three Fountains to the west, with a waterfall created by the incline of the ground, and the Grove of the Triumphal Arch to the east.

In the latter, water gushed from a gilded metal arch at the top of the slope, and a little farther down the sides stood the Fountains of Glory and Victory. Finally, opposite the Triumphal Arch, rose the majestic gilt lead group of "France in Triumph", the work of Tuby and Coysevox, of which only an impressive trace now remains in the abandoned grove.

F. Girardon's Pyramid, "a little temple to the glory of water"

The gardens
of the
Petit Trianon

210

TRIANON

The Marble
Trianon:
front of the north wing

212

The Grand Trianon

In 1668, Louis XIV, having decided to enlarge his domains, bought a small village, called Trianon, situated at the edge of Versailles. He then asked his architect, Le Vau, to build on this site a pavilion which would serve as a meeting-place for all kinds of rustic festivities.

In 1670 the House of Porcelain was completed; it was a small building and the outside was entirely decorated with blue-and-white Delft pottery tiles. But this little château was fragile and also proved too small for the King. In 1687, Louis XIV commissioned J.H. Mansart to design a new dwelling which would be on a more royal scale; and it was a veritable palace that the Sun King finally inaugurated in 1688, in the company of the Grand Dauphin and Madame de Maintenon. This was the Marble Trianon that we know today.

The Main Gateway

Furniture by Jacob-Desmalter
and blue figured silk
created for Marie-Antoinette

The Main Courtyard is flanked by two wings linked by a gallery opening onto the gardens. The walls of the façades, in white stone, are decorated with pink marble pilasters; the balustrade crowning the buildings was adorned, until the Revolution, with vases, trophies and groups of children. As soon as it was completed the Grand Trianon became the setting for festivities in honour of the royal family.

At Louis XIV's death, the château was deserted for many years, for Louis XV and Louis XVI took little interest in the Grand Trianon. During the Revolution, the furnishings were sold but the château survived. In 1805, Napoleon ordered it to be restored and refurnished. Under Louis-Philippe, a little life once more returned to the Trianon, as he often stayed there with his family.

Then, for almost a century, it slipped into oblivion, until 1962 when General de Gaulle, President of the Republic, decided to use the palace for receptions in honour of foreign Heads of State.

The Council Chamber
or Mirror
Drawing-Room

It was then that colossal restoration work was undertaken to save the Trianon from the threat of decay and give it new life. Since the furniture of the period had gone, it was impossible to reconstruct the Louis XIV settings. What we see now is the Grand Trianon as Napoleon and Louis-Philippe knew it. A search was made for the furniture, chandeliers and objets d'art of this time and many were found and returned to their original places. The curtains, carpets and silks were rewoven after original models.

The south wing held the Sun King's first apartments, later occupied, in 1703, by his son, the Grand Dauphin. The furnishings were renovated in 1805 for Madame Mère and, in 1810, it was Empress Marie-Louise who moved here. Under the July Monarchy, Louis-Philippe often stayed in these rooms.

The first three rooms, on the site of what were formerly antechambers, are decorated with paintings and furniture from palaces which had been destroyed. A gallery leads us to Marie-Louise's Boudoir, furnished with a "triumphal arch" writing-desk which once belonged to Josephine.

The Mirror Drawing-Room, once Louis XIV's Council Chamber, was used as a State reception room by the later occupants of the suite. The decoration consists of arched mirrors alternating with rectangular ones and fine sculptures, including the cornice adorned with children, a symbol of war and peace. The curtains of blue figured silk representing the four corners of the earth were created for Marie-Antoinette. The seats, consoles and small tables are the work of Jacob-Desmalter. The Bedchamber which follows was lived in by Louis XIV, then by the Grand Dauphin, later by Marie-Louise in 1810 and, in 1836, by Louis-Philippe and Marie-Amélie; it is their furniture which is here today.

The Chapel Antechamber was originally the Chapel of the Grand Trianon, and its restrained decoration results from its first use — the cornice carved with

The Peristyle
of the Grand Trianon
by Robert de Cotte

216

ears of corn and bunches of grapes symbolizes the bread and wine of Holy Communion. The final room in this wing is the Antechamber of the Courtiers.

The Peristyle by Robert de Cotte, which stands on the site of the first Porcelain Trianon, is a kind of covered terrace linking the wings of the palace without blocking the view from the Main Courtyard to the gardens.

The first room of the large suite in the north wing, the Round Room with its set of Corinthian columns, is one of Mansart's finest creations at Trianon. During recent restoration work the marble mosaïc pavement, removed by Louis-Philippe, was reconstructed.

Beyond the Music Room, the Family Room was created by Louis-Philippe on the site of two earlier rooms used by Louis XIV as an antechamber and bedroom. This room has been furnished so as to evoke the atmosphere of those intimate family gatherings, and includes the tables with numbered drawers in which the princesses kept their needlework.

The Cabinet du Couchant, or Emperor's Grand Cabinet, was formerly the Sun King's Grand Cabinet. Napoleon placed here the malachite furniture that was a gift from the Czar Alexander I after their talks at Tilsit. The chairs are covered with crimson damask with an oak-leaf design, embellished with gold thread. The carpet bears the names of Apollo and the Muses, with their symbols.

The Salon Frais, a council chamber during the Empire, contains some furniture from the Napoleonic period, but the decoration is still that chosen by Louis XIV. The great paintings in their original frames were intended by Mansart to form part of the decorative ensemble created by this room and the Gallery linking the north wing with Trianon-in-the-Woods. These paintings depict the groves of the Versailles gardens, many of which are gone.

The Peristyle
seen from the
Grand Trianon gardens

The
Cabinet
du Couchant

219

The Garden Drawing-Room was first used as a games room. Converted into a billiards room by Louis XV, it links the Gallery with the wing known as Trianon-in-the-Woods, built in stone without a veneer of marble, and intended for the children of the royal family.

Madame de Maintenon's apartments, looking east onto the King's Garden became the Emperor's apartments. In the first room, the Room of the Springs, Napoleon I set up his Map Room. From here, an antechamber led to the Emperor's Study. Next to this room is the Bathroom, then the Bedchamber, with its buff and lilac silk fabrics embroidered with silver thread; the Breakfast Parlour completes this suite, a testimony to the private life of the Emperor.

The front section which runs along the main courtyard contained a little theatre until 1703. Louis XIV then made this his third apartment, which was later used by Louis XV and Napoleon I as a reception suite. Under Louis-Philippe it became the apartments of the King and Queen of the Belgians. The famous chests designed by Boulle, which today are in the Salon de Mercure at Versailles, were made around 1708 for the Sun King's bedchamber here.

The upper garden
and the Gallery
wing

The
Garden
Drawing-Room

The steps from
the Garden
Drawing-Room

For Louis XIV, the gardens of Trianon, like those of all his residences, had an essential rôle to play. Those of Versailles are inspired by a whole mythological symbolism; there is nothing of the kind at Trianon — the garden is a simple, but remarkable, homage to nature itself.

Although it was badly treated towards the end of the eighteenth century, the original layout of the garden has been preserved, with its parterres, its woods and its two smaller gardens, the Garden of Springs and the King's Garden.

The flower parterres still retain the broad outlines laid out at the time of the Porcelain Trianon with its Upper and Lower Gardens. They were altered by Le Nôtre who worked on them until his death in 1700.

The Garden of Springs is unfortunately no more than a large lawn. It was once "a delightful little wood which the sun could scarcely penetrate...". As for the King's Garden, it was given attentive care and was "full of flowers that were changed each season".

The façade overlooking
the upper garden
of the Grand Trianon

223

The Petit Trianon

In 1761, Louis XV commissioned Gabriel to create, to the north-east of the Grand Trianon, a pavilion in which he could live in the midst of the gardens he supervised with such loving care.

Madame de Pompadour encouraged the King in his project, but she died in 1764, and the Petit Trianon was not completed until four more years had passed.

After the death of Louis XV, Louis XVI gave this architectural jewel to Marie-Antoinette in 1774, as she longed to live far from the burden of court etiquette. Unfortunately, the Queen was not interested in Louis XV's scientific work. The botanical garden and hothouses in which the King had raised fig-trees, coffee-shrubs and pineapples were destroyed and, on the site, an Anglo-Chinese garden in the fashion of the time was laid out by Mique and Hubert Robert.

Portico and steps
of the façade
facing the French Pavilion

The Petit Trianon,
the masterpiece
by Ange-Jacques Gabriel

This little château is without a doubt Gabriel's masterpiece. For the pleasure of his King he made this small pavilion a model of harmony and elegance imitated throughout the entire world.

Built on a square ground-plan, the building consists of a basement, a main floor and an attic storey crowned with a balustrade which hides a flat roof. Due to the different levels of the ground the basement is visible only from the Main Courtyard and the Temple of Love. Each of the four façades is different — pilasters on the courtyard side, columns and steps facing the French Pavilion and a plain façade overlooking the park. The Main Courtyard is enclosed by a low railing flanked by two elegant stone sentry boxes. On the left are the outbuildings and the chapel.

Once finished, the Petit Trianon was of little use to those who had wanted it. Madame de Pompadour, whose idea it had been, died before work was completed and Louis XV, during his stay there with Madame du Barry in April 1774, felt the first attacks of the terrible disease that was to end his life. Marie-Antoinette, who was only nineteen at the time, was delighted to own a house where she could live in "simple privacy". It soon became her favorite residence, and was furnished in the "modern" style she loved.

After work on the main floor has been completed, it is hoped that the basement and attic apartments will also be restored. Visitors will then find an intimate dwelling still filled with the atmosphere of the eighteenth century.

The staircase of subdued elegance leads us to the first floor apartments. Its wrought iron balustrade bearing the Queen's monogram stands out against the golden stone of the walls.

Façade with pilasters
overlooking the Main
Courtyard

The Petit
Trianon
staircase

The landing is adorned with carvings by Guibert and over the stairwell hangs an admirable round lantern hung there in 1811 by order of the Emperor.

The door on the right leads to the antechamber. This room was once furnished with painted wooden seats covered with a crimson velvet-pile fabric, and, on either side of the door leading to the Dining-Room, stood two faïence stoves.

The following room, the Dining-Room, has recently been restored to its original state. One can now admire the superb panelling by Guibert with flowers, fruit and foliage painted white on a pale green background. The paintings commissioned by Louis XV showing scenes of fishing, the hunt, the harvest and the wine harvest once more frame the doors opposite each other. The overdoors portray the gods of fruit and flowers. The chairs by Sené come from Louis XVI's games room in the château of Compiègne and the two ebony sideboards are from the furniture in the Tuileries.

This room opens onto Louis XV's small dining-room named the "cabinet overlooking the flower-garden", after the garden outside. Marie-Antoinette made it her billiards room. Crimson silk is used for curtains and to cover the chairs by Dupain. The Riesener commode bears the stamp of the Queen's Furniture

The Dining-Room
and "cabinet overlooking
the flower garden"

The fireplace
in the Grand
Drawing-Room

Repository. The wall-sconces, andirons and clock are from the Louis XVI period.

The wood-panelling in the Grand Drawing-Room is among the finest carved by Guibert for these rooms. The recently completed restoration revealed the quality of this work — the two intertwined L's in the midst of realistic fleurs-de-lis, obliterated during the Revolution, were rediscovered in the medallions at the foot of the panels. The triple-colored crimson damask, like that of the Queen's time, and the furniture, including the magnificent Riesener writing-desk, which was placed here by Empress Eugénie, conjure up perfectly this lost art of living in simplicity and calm which was practiced at Trianon.

Marie-Antoinette converted Louis XV's study into her bedchamber and the wainscoting carved with flowers dates from Louis XV's time. It reminds us of his love for the botanical garden onto which the windows of this room opened. Certain pieces were commissioned by the Queen for this room, and among these are the clock with eaglets by Robin and the chairs from the famous furniture richly carved with floral motifs delivered by Jacob in 1787. From this suite only two armchairs, two chairs, a stool and a firescreen remain. The chairs still have their original coverings, a very rare phenomenon; this is an English cotton damask woven by Desfarges and embroidered with flowers of colored wool.

The Boudoir, a delightful room behind the bedchamber, was entirely renovated for Marie-Antoinette. Its wainscoting, with fine arabesques bearing the Queen's monogram, is certainly the work of the architect Mique. When these delicate carvings have been restored, the "moving mirrors", which could be made to cover the windows, can be placed here again.

The Cabinet de Toilette still has some souvenirs of the time, such as the portrait of the Dauphin, Louis XVII, by Kucharski and the ivory clock made for Marie-Antoinette by Louis XV himself.

The
Grand Drawing-Room
in the Petit Trianon

Marie-Antoinette shared the taste of her time for the theatre and dreamed of having her own theatre in the grounds of Trianon. Her architect, R. Mique, completed the construction of the simple building in 1780. Only the entrance porch, with sculpture on the pediment by Deschamps, can be seen from the outside, but the interior decor of papier-mâché is quite sumptuous. Above the stage is a cartouche bearing the Queen's monogram, supported by two nymphs. The ceiling by Lagrenée having been destroyed, Monsieur Pierre Paulet made a replica after the original design.

The performances were held in private, the actors and audience being none other than the Queen, the members of the royal family and a few servants. This is how little comic operas, such as ''The Village Soothsayer'', by Jean-Jacques Rousseau, were performed.

Marie-Antoinette's
theatre by
Richard Mique

The French Pavilion was built by Gabriel in 1750 so that the King could rest during his long visits to his botanical garden. It is a small building with a cross-shaped ground-plan. Four rectangular cabinets radiate from a large round drawing-room. The façade is very simple: only the groups of children and the vases decorating the roof balustrade show the influence of rococo architecture. The richly decorated interior makes a strong contrast. In the drawing-room the floor of colored marble and the walls decorated with wainscoting by Verberckt create a remarkable ensemble.

To the north-west of the theatre lies the landscape garden dear to Marie-Antoinette. On the banks of an artificial lake, a rock is the foundation for the Belvedere, an octagonal building in the neoclassical style, the work of Mique, reached by four steps flanked by sphinxes. The door pediments are ornamented with hunting motifs and the relief carvings over the tall windows symbolize the four seasons.

The French Pavilion between the Grand and Petit Trianon

The Belvedere between the Petit Trianon and the Queen's Hamlet

The Queen's Hamlet

As one walks along the winding paths of the park one comes upon Marie-Antoinette's Grotto. A short distance away is the former Orangery and then the house of Claude Richard, the gardener. Further along the river lies the Great Lake, the banks of which are dotted with the buildings of the Queen's Hamlet.

Marie-Antoinette's Hamlet is a little village of cottages with cob walls and thatched roofs, inspired by those built for the Prince de Condé in the park of the château of Chantilly. Work on the hamlet was directed by Mique and begun in 1783.

Portrait of Marie-Antoinette
with a rose,
by Mme E. L. Vigée-Lebrun

Each cottage served a precise purpose; two have gone — the Preparation Dairy and the Barn, which was also used as a ballroom, were destroyed during the First Empire.

If the wanderer walks along the left bank of the lake his steps lead him to the Processing Dairy and the Marlborough Tower with the Fishery in its basement, and, a little further on, to the Farmhouse, recognizable by its large main door decorated with reliefs.

Returning along the avenue one passes the Guardian's House (at the time, the guardian was the Swiss, Bersy), then the Dovecot with its charming staircase and, after crossing a little bridge, one finally reaches the Queen's House, the principal construction in the Hamlet. In fact, it consists of two buildings linked by a rustic arcade — the Queen's House and the Billiards House. It is reached by an exterior spiral staircase decorated with faïence flower-pots with Marie-Antoinette's monogram. The now empty rooms were decorated for Empress Marie-Louise and all the cottages in the Hamlet were refurnished at that time; some of the furnishings still remain. Behind the Queen's House are the Boudoir and the Réchauffoir which served as kitchen and pantry. The last thatched building in the Hamlet is the Mill. It still has its wheel which, alas, no longer turns.

The Great Lake
and the Hamlet
of Trianon

By continuing beyond the Mill, along the path to the Petit Trianon, we pass by the Temple of Love, which stands in the center of an islet where the river divides. Built in 1778, it consists of a circular base of six steps on which rise twelve Corinthian columns of white marble holding a cupola. In the center we see "Love carving his bow from Hercules' club", a replica, made for Madame de Pompadour, of the statue carved by Bouchardon in 1746. The original is at present in the Louvre.

And so we regretfully leave this domain which became legendary when the last of the Queens of France, the youngest, flightiest and most beautiful of the Queens of Versailles, made this her favorite dwelling in June 1774. It was here that, fifteen years later, the approaching upheaval of the Revolution took her by surprise. In Autumn 1789, Marie-Antoinette abandoned Trianon for the suffering which awaited her as her tragic fate was fulfilled.

The Mill
on a June
evening

The Temple
of Love
in October

Great Occasions at Versailles

Louis XIV's genius was to have created a work capable of being a continuous source of inspiration in all the artistic and technical fields during the whole of the eighteenth century in Europe. The incomparable strength of Versailles in comparison with other monuments of antiquity and the modern world comes from its capacity for change — it is a living universe. Logic and reason compel one to strive so that the Palace of the Sun may never cease to dazzle mankind, despite the ravages of time. To desire the rediscovery of Versailles with the glory of its past is to be modern. For this past is one of the most glittering pages in the history of humanity.

The 6th October 1789 is a major turning-point in the history of Versailles. After the departure of the King, the château was stripped and became an enormous building whose upkeep was ruinously expensive. And so a long period of uncertainty and peril began. Some members of the National Convention demanded its complete destruction, like the royal residences at Marly and Choisy-le-Roi. All the obstinacy and fierce opposition of the inhabitants of Versailles were needed to remove this death threat. On 5th May 1794, the Convention decreed that the upkeep of the former royal domains of Versailles would henceforth be at the Republic's expense "to serve for the festivities of the People and create establishments useful for agriculture and the arts". Two years earlier a small section of the palace had already been set aside to hold the objets d'art which had been seized in the region.

So the memorable occasions at Versailles, begun under Louis XIII, did not end with the fall of the legitimate monarchy but continue to this day (despite the pillaging of the château's art works and their removal to the Louvre in Paris — a traffic which ended only under Louis-Philippe and later began again, continuing until the first half of the 20th century).

Versailles was visited and restored by Napoleon I and Louis XVIII who saved the palace from ruin. But the credit for having given Versailles significance in the modern world must go to Louis-Philippe, who installed the Museum of French History there.

This Museum, opened on 10th June 1837, is dedicated "To all the Glories of France". Since this date its collections have continued to grow. It was after the Second World War that the renaissance of Versailles took place, thanks to the Conservation law of 1953.

Detail from C. G. Hallé's "Audience for the Doge of Genoa", showing the Hall of Mirrors in 1685

Since then, the Directors of Versailles have renovated Louis-Philippe's exhibition (while nevertheless leaving intact some sections such as the Hall of Battles, the Rooms of the Crusades and the Empire Rooms on the ground-floor of the South Wing). Since 1953, too, the main building of the palace has again been given its appearance of a royal residence. Most of the rooms have been restored to their former state. The last room to be completed was the Queen's Bedchamber, restored as Marie-Antoinette knew it on the sad day of her departure on the afternoon of 6th October 1789. Soon the Hall of Mirrors, the King's Bedchamber and the Queen's apartments in the Petit Trianon will be shown to the public in their former splendour.

Many works have been dedicated to the history of Versailles, to its creation by Louis XIV who made it the seat of the French government and to the Court life of the seventeenth and eighteenth centuries, but the author considered it useful to recall on the following pages the chronology of its great hours and memorable events from its origins to our time.

"The King governs alone"
by Charles Le Brun: detail from
the ceiling of the Hall of Mirrors

1075 First mention of the name of Versailles in Philippe I's "Book of Records".

1275 Gilles, Baron of Versailles, relinquishes his rights to Trianon to the Abbé of Saint-Germain.

1607 The Dauphin, the future Louis XIII, goes on his first hunt at Versailles.

1624 Louis XIII orders a hunting lodge to be built on the Versailles hill.

1630 On 1st November, Cardinal Richelieu goes to Versailles in secret and succeeds in gaining the King's confidence. The Queen Mother is disgraced; this is the "Day of the Dupes". Richelieu remains Prime Minister and Marie de Medicis goes into exile.

1631 Louis XIII has the hunting lodge destroyed. On its site, Philibert Le Roy builds a small brick and stone palace. Work is completed in 1634. Boyceau and Menours lay out the gardens.

1643 Louis XIII's last stay at Versailles. He dies on 14th May.

1651 Louis XIV's first visit. The King is twelve years of age.

1660 On 17th June, Louis XIV marries his cousin, the Infanta Marie-Thérèse of Austria. The royal couple go to Versailles on 25th October.

1661 Beginning of Louis XIV's passion for Versailles. Death of the Prime Minister, Cardinal Mazarin. Beginning of the personal reign. J.B. Colbert is appointed Superintendent of Finances. Birth of the Grand Dauphin.

1662 First large-scale renovation of the château, decoration of the gardens and reconstruction of the former outbuildings: one million, five hundred thousand *livres* are spent in less than a year despite Colbert's stubborn opposition.

1663 Louis Le Vau builds the first Orangery and begins the Menagerie.

1664 In May, the King holds the festivities called "The Pleasures of the Enchanted Island" including the first performances of Molière's "The Princess of Elis" and "Tartuffe".

1665 The first statues are placed in the park. Construction of the grotto of Tethys is begun.

1666 Death of the Queen Mother, Anne of Austria. The King and Queen withdraw to Versailles where they receive a visit from the Queen of England.

1667 The Grand Canal, the continuation of the east-west view, is begun.

1668 Adoption of Louis Le Vau's project to enlarge the château on the garden side by constructing a "stone envelope". On 18th July, to the amazement of the whole of Europe, Louis XIV holds the most memorable celebration ever to take place at Versailles: "The Great Royal Entertainment". For this occasion Molière writes "Georges Dandin" and Lully "Les Fêtes de l'Amour et de Bacchus".

1670 Creation of the Porcelain Trianon. On 20th June, death of "Madame", Henrietta of England, Duchesse d'Orléans, the King's sister-in-law and daughter of Charles I of England. In July, visit by the Duke of Buckingham. Death of Le Vau.

1671 Le Vau's "stone envelope" is completed. Decoration of the State Apartments begins. New statues for the gardens.

1672 Creation of the sumptuous Appartement des Bains.

1673 Visit by the Duchess of York, wife of the future King James II of England.

1674 Year of the "great commission" of the 24 marble statues designed by Le Brun. The last of the three great celebrations at Versailles, with works by Molière, Lully and Racine (in July and August).

From
'1075
to 1686

1675 Reception for the Duchess of Tuscany at Versailles.

1677 Louis XIV reveals his intention of making Versailles his residence.

1678 Signature of the treaties of Nimeguen. When peace was restored, Jules Hardouin-Mansart was commissioned to undertake new construction work. Building of the Hall of Mirrors. The South Wing and Lake of the Swiss Guards are begun.

1679 Reception for the new Queen of Spain, Mademoiselle d'Orléans, after her recent marriage to Charles II. Construction of the Great and Small Stables on the Place d'Armes and completion of the Ministers' Wings.

1681 Construction of the "Marly Machine". Charles Le Brun and his team complete decoration of the State Apartments. The King receives the ambassadors of the Grand Duke of Muscovy, Potemkin and Polskow.

1682 On 6th May, Louis XIV decrees that Versailles is henceforth to be his residence and seat of the Court and Government. Birth of the Duc de Bourgogne.

1683 On 30th July, death of Queen Marie-Thérèse. On 19th December, birth of the Duc d'Anjou, the Sun King's grandson, who was to become Philip V of Spain. The "Milon of Croton" by Puget is placed at the entrance to the Tapis Vert.

1684 Completion of the Hall of Mirrors. Construction of the new Orangery and flight of the Hundred Steps.

1685 Audience for the Algerian delegates. On 15th May, an extraordinary audience for Francesco Lercaro, the Doge of Genoa. On 21st May, audience for the Muscovite ambassadors. Puget's "Perseus and Andromeda" is placed at the entrance to the Tapis Vert. Work is begun on the North Wing and the Colonnade.

1686 Reception for the Siamese ambassadors. Delivery of the solid silver furniture for the State Apartments.

Great
Occasions
at Versailles

1687 To replace the Porcelain Trianon, J. H.-Mansart builds a new palace, the Marble Trianon.

1689 On 8th January, reception for King James II of England. In December, Louis XIV orders the royal silverware and silver furniture to be melted down.

1697 The Duc de Bourgogne marries Marie-Adélaïde of Savoy.

1699 On 16th February, audience for the ambassadors of the King of Morocco. Mansart begins work on the new royal chapel between the main building of the palace and the North Wing. Girardon's "Rape of Persephone by Pluto" is placed in the Colonnade.

1700 On 16th November, the Duc d'Anjou becomes King Philip V of Spain.

1704 Visit by Carlo Gonzaga, the Duke of Mantua.

1706 Reception for Joseph Clement of Bavaria, the Elector of Cologne.

1710 On 15th February, birth of the Duc d'Anjou, the future Louis XV. On 4th March, reception for the Elector of Bavaria. Consecration of the new Chapel on 5th June.

1711 Death of the Grand Dauphin at Meudon. His son, the Duc de Bourgogne, becomes heir to the throne.

1712 Death of the Duc and Duchesse de Bourgogne, the Dauphin and Dauphine of France, in February, within several days of each other, as well as of their eldest son. The Duc d'Anjou becomes Dauphin. The Salon d'Hercule is begun.

1713 Visit by the Elector of Cologne and the Elector of Bavaria.

1715 On 19th February, extraordinary audience for Mehemet Riza-Beg, the Persian ambassador. On 1st September, at 8:15 in the morning, death of Louis XIV. On 9th September, Louis XV moves from Versailles to Vincennes and then to Paris.

1717 Peter the Great, Czar of Russia, stays in the Grand Trianon.

1722 Louis XV returns in June to make Versailles his residence.

1725 On 5th September at Fontainebleau, marriage of the King and Maria Leczinska, the daughter of Stanislas, ex-King of Poland.

1729 Birth of the Dauphin. Audience for the envoys from Tripoli. New decoration for the Queen's bedchamber.

1736 Pope Clement XII presents Maria Leczinska with the "Golden Rose". Opening of the Salon d'Hercule.

1738 Renovation of the King's Private Suite begins.

1742 On 11th January, extraordinary audience for the ambassador of the Sultan in the Hall of Mirrors.

1745 Marriage of the Dauphin to the Infanta of Spain who dies the following year.

1747 Marriage of the Dauphin to Marie-Josèphe of Saxony.

1750 Gabriel builds the French Pavilion at Trianon.

1752 Louis XV orders the destruction of the Ambassador's Staircase.

1754 On 23rd August, birth of the Duc de Berry, the future Louis XVI.

1755 Gabriel redecorates the King's Council Chamber.

1757 On 5th January, attack on Louis XV by Damiens.

1758 Treaty of Versailles between France and Austria.

1764 Death of Madame de Pompadour at the château of Versailles.

1765 The Dauphin (father of Louis XVI, Louis XVIII and Charles X) dies at Fontainebleau.

1768 Death of Queen Maria Leczinska on 25th June. Reception for Christian VII of Denmark on 21st November. Completion of the Petit Trianon.

1770 On 11th April, Madame Louise de France enters the Carmelite order at Saint-Denis. On 16th May, celebration of the Dauphin's marriage to Marie-Antoinette of Austria-Lorraine and completion of the Opera House built by Gabriel.

1774 On 10th May, death of Louis XV at Versailles. Louis XVI orders the park to be replanted and a new library built.

1777 Reception for Joseph II of Austria, the Queen's brother.

1778 On 20th May, the King receives a delegation of American insurgents led by Benjamin Franklin, Silas Deane and Arthur Lee. Mique begins construction of Marie-Antoinette's theatre at Trianon.

1781 On 29th July, Joseph II's second visit. On 22nd October, birth of the Dauphin. Creation of the Cabinet de la Méridienne.

1782 On 20th May, Louis XVI's reception for the Grand Duke of Russia.

1783 In January and September, signature of the treaties confirming the independence of the United States of America. Construction of the Queen's Hamlet by Mique.

1784 Reception for the King of Sweden, Gustave III, on 7th June, under the name of the Count of Haga. On 23rd June in the Great Courtyard, Pilâtre de Rozier flies in a hot-air balloon.

1785 On 27th March, birth of the Duc de Normandie, the future Louis XVII. On 15th August, the affair of the "Queen's Necklace" breaks out.

1787 The Assembly of Notables opens on 22nd February.

1788 Reception for the Ambassadors of Tippo-Sahib in the Salon d'Hercule.

1789 On 5th May, the assembly of the Estates General opens. On 4th June, death of the Dauphin. On 14th July, the storming of the Bastille. On 26th August, declaration of the "Rights of Man and the Citizen". On 6th October, the château is invaded by the Parisians and the King leaves Versailles.

From
1770
to the present

1792 and 1793 Sale of the royal furniture. Temporary creation of the Museum of the French School. On 21st January 1793, Louis XVI is decapitated and the Queen is executed on 16th October.

1805 Visit by Pope Pius VII. Under the Empire and Restoration, work is undertaken to restore the royal domain.

1833 to 1837 Louis-Philippe commissions work to begin on the Museum of French History, which is inaugurated on 10th June 1837.

1855 Reception for Queen Victoria, Queen of England.

1871 On 18th January, proclamation of the German Empire in the Hall of Mirrors. The National Assembly holds its sessions in the Opera House.

1875 The architect, E. de Joly, builds the Congress Room (used for the election of the President of the Republic) in the South Wing.

1919 On 28th June, the Allies and Germany sign the treaty putting an end to the First World War.

1953 Adoption of the law safeguarding Versailles, which saved the domain from ruin.

1957 Adoption of the "Debré Decree", stipulating that all the masterpieces which once belonged to Versailles be returned there. Reopening of the restored Opera House in the presence of Queen Elizabeth II of England.

1962 General de Gaulle orders the Grand Trianon to be restored and used as a residence for France's official guests. From 1963 to 1975, a large number of receptions are held for foreign sovereigns and Heads of State.

1975 Reopening of the Queen's Bedchamber, restored thanks to generous donations, and of the Petit Trianon Drawing-Rooms, thanks to M. Valéry Giscard d'Estaing.

ACKNOWLEDGEMENTS

France is most appreciative of all the friendships Versailles has won and is particularly grateful to the many French and foreign donors who, through their generosity, have greatly contributed to the prestige of Versailles by helping to enlarge its collections and have brought about its resurrection.

In 1923, John D. Rockefeller led the way by taking over the cost of repairing the roof of the Hall of Mirrors and the restoration of all the statues in the park and of Marie-Antoinette's Hamlet. His work was continued by his children who, after the war, saw to the reconstruction of the Grand Trianon roof. Their efforts were then continued by the Ambassadors Messrs David Bruce and Douglas Dillon, to whom we owe the restoration of the Petit Trianon staircase.

More recently, the Dauphin's Bedchamber has been given a new lease of life through the superb furniture donated by the Comte du Boisrouvray and his daughter Albina. Its former glory has been restored to the Queen's Bedchamber thanks to the Kress Foundation, Mr Graham Mattison, Miss Barbara Hutton, Princess Na Champaçak and M. Pierre David-Weill. The King's Bedchamber is being restored through the combined efforts of M. Arturo Lopez Willshaw, Miss Barbara Hutton, Princess Na Champaçak and M. Pierre Schlumberger. Another legendary part of Versailles, the Hall of Mirrors, will soon be able to shine with all its lights due to the decisive help of Mr and Mrs William Levitt and the generosity of Mr and Mrs Robert Magowan, Mr George Parker Jr and Mr and Mrs Charles Lachmann.

The creation, several years ago, of the Versailles Foundation was a determining factor. Permission was generously granted by the American Government and the Foundation was created and developed under the patronage of the Ambassador, Mr Arthur Watson, Mr Douglas Dillon, Mrs Albert Lasker, M Pierre David Weill, Mr Daniel Wildenstein and Mme Gérald Van der Kemp.

It would be impossible to describe here all that Versailles owes to each of its friends; in homage to all, we should like to mention some of the Museum's great donors: the Rockefeller family, Mme Léon Barzin, Sir Alfred and Lady Beit, Mme Fédérico Bemberg, M Marcel Bissey, M. Edgar Brandt and the House of Brandt, M. et Mme Paul Derval, M. Edmond Dreyfus and his sister, Mme Sély, Mme Henri Goldet, Mrs Florence Gould, a magnificent friend of Versailles, M. César de Haucke, Mrs Ira Haupt, Mrs Stewart Hooker, Mrs Melville Hall, H.E. Mr Walter Annenberg, Mr William McCormick Blair Sr., Mr and Mrs Bernard Combemale, Mr Nathan Cummings, Mr and Mrs Rushmore Kress, the Marquis and Marquise de La Ferronays, Mrs Arturo Lopez Willshaw, Mr and Mrs Joseph Lauder, Mr and Mrs Irvin Levy, Dr Franklin Murphy, Mrs O'Neil Ryan, Mr and Mrs Jules Stein, Mr and Mrs William Wood Prince, Mrs Charles Munn, Mrs Richard Lounsberry, Mme Ethel de Croisset, Mr George Frelinghausen, Mrs Dolly Green, Mr and Mrs Harding Lawrence, Mr and Mrs Proctor Jones, Miss Jayne Teagle, Mr Henry Ford, Comte and Comtesse Niel, Comte Anne-Jules de Noailles, Comtesse Georges de Pimodan, Baron de Rédé, Baron Edmond de Rothschild, M. Jean Thoman and the Taco Company, Comtesse Vigier, Comte and Comtesse Roger Walewski, Commandant Paul-Louis Weiller, Baronne Guy de Rothschild, Vicomtesse de Bonchamps, M. Baudouin Dierckx de Casterlé, Chevalier Kraft de la Saulx, M. Antenor Patino, M. Henri Samuel, Dr Roudinesco... and how can we express our thanks to all those innumerable friends like the Duc de Brissac and the Société des Amis de Versailles, the Conseil National du Patronat Français, Baronne Elie de Rothschild, the Duc and Duchesse de Mouchy, who gave us their help and encouragement with such generous enthusiasm and whose incomparable moral and material support we so gratefully appreciate.

Selected reading List

The following list is in no way intended to be comprehensive and includes only modern works on the creation of Versailles, together with a few works giving the social and political background of the times. Many of the books listed here include comprehensive bibliographies, to which the reader is referred for further information.

BARRY, Joseph, *Versailles: the Passions and Politics of an Era*. London, 1972. (Published in the USA under the title *Passions and Politics: a biography of Versailles*, New York, 1972.)

BLUNT, Anthony, *Art and Architecture in France 1500 to 1700*. Harmondsworth and New York, 1953, revised 1970.

MARIE, Alfred, *Naissance de Versailles*. 2 vols, Paris, 1968.
— *Mansart à Versailles*. 2 vols, Paris, 1972.
— *Versailles au temps de Louis XIV*. Paris, 1976.

MAURICHEAU-BEAUPRÉ, Charles, *Versailles, l'histoire et l'art - Guide officiel*. Paris, 1955.

MITFORD, Nancy, *The Sun King*. London and New York, 1966.

NOLHAC, Pierre de, *La création de Versailles*. Paris, 1925.
— *Versailles, résidence de Louis XIV*. Paris, 1925.
— *Versailles au xviiie siècle*. Paris, 1926.
— *Trianon*, Paris, 1927.
— *Louis XV et Marie Leczinska*. Paris, 1928.
— *Louis XV et Madame de Pompadour*. Paris, 1928.
— *Marie-Antoinette Dauphine*. Paris, 1929.
— *La reine Marie-Antoinette*. Paris, 1929.
— *Madame de Pompadour et la politique*. Paris, 1930.
— *L'Art à Versailles*. Paris, 1930.

Revue du Louvre et des Musées de France, No. 3 on Versailles. Paris, 1976.

SAINT-SIMON, Louis de Rouvroy, Duc de, *Historical Memoirs of the duc de Saint-Simon: a shortened version*, edited and translated by Lucy Norton. Vol. I: 1691-1709; Vol. II: 1710-1715; Vol. III: 1715-1723. London and New York, 1967-1972.
(Several shorter selections from the *Memoirs* have been published, including *Louis XIV at Versailles*, translated and edited by Desmond Flower, London, 1953; and *Saint-Simon at Versailles*, selected and translated by Lucy Norton with preface by Nancy Mitford, London, 1958.)

SOULIE, Eudore, *Notice du Musée National de Versailles*. 3 vols, Paris, 1880.

VAN der KEMP, Gérald, *Versailles et Trianon, description générale - guide officiel*. Versailles, 1975.

VERLET, Pierre, *Versailles*. Paris, 1961.

ZIEGLER, Gilette, *The Court of Versailles: Eyewitness Reports from the Reign of Louis XIV*, translated by Simon Watson Taylor. London and New York, 1966.

Index

Note. Furniture-making in France during the period covered by this book was a highly specialized activity, governed by strict guild rules limiting each craftsman to the practice of one particular technique. Thus members of four or more different guilds could be involved in the creation of a single piece of furniture. There is no equivalent sub-division in English, and it has therefore been thought best to leave the names of the different trades in the original French. For guidance only, *menuisier* corresponds roughly to carpenter and joiner, and *ébéniste* to cabinet-maker. Bronze work was the responsibility of the *fondeur*, who cast the piece, and the *ciseleur*, who finished it.

The addition of the letter 'c' after a page reference = caption.